Americunt

Author: Matthew Garon

Editor: Melissa Garon

Dedications

This book is primarily dedicated to the sick, suffering, gleaming, flourishing addict, and struggling parent. Also, to my family; Tammy, Evelyn, Mom, Dad, Michael, Melissa, Emily, Thomas, Olivia, and James. You are my connection and purpose.

1 | Americunt

An evolutionary breakdown in ethics and parenting from the eyes of a former meth addict

<u>Americunt</u>

Noun:

1.) Anyone whose actions prove to protect self-image over human decency.

2.) Humans who blindly believe that their intentions are equally as valid as their actions.

3.) Those that go to endless lengths to protect themselves regardless of culpability.

4.) Those who have a seemingly allergic reaction to the words "I was wrong."

5.) Those who have two feet firmly planted in the listening just means waiting to speak club.

6.) Those who believe it's more important to know about everything else before oneself.

April 15th, 2013, the day of the marathon bombings in Boston, my hometown capital, marked the day of my enlightenment to evolutionary regression sparked by my own physical re-matriculation to my area of birth. The previous six years of the slobbery of an existence I lived were spent working gainfully throughout Southeast Asia, where the beauty of the human soul burns brighter than an aurora. Granted, there is no economic and technological revolution going on in Thailand or the Philippines…and that is exactly the answer. There is much less of an implied race to achieved success in Asian cultures. I'm not here to be some pontificating clown explaining to Americans about how technology has ruined us and our children. There is a huge resource in our abilities as humans to advance technologically, but that resource has clouded superlative minds and their abilities to differentiate themselves from their intentions, and to be compassionate and meek. **Just because we can do something, does it mean that we are obligated to?**

Americans seem to attach negative connotations to the words meek, humility, and compassion. We need each other less and we make sure everyone knows it. The ease and comfort of dealing with ourselves is reason enough for most Western civilizations to push forward as dismissive *Americunts*. Personally, I am no better a person than anyone on Earth, but I can recognize the differences in levels of compassion, sincerity, and willingness in people. That's clear to anyone, and clearly a lost virtue on American soil. The real-time grossness of our culture is one where our cohorts and peers identify failure aggressively in others in order to promote themselves. It's considered widely acceptable to provide personal attestations of other's failures to self-promote. See something, say something... Our leaders have convinced us of our important roles as law-abiding citizens. It's now not what you can do, but what others didn't do or cannot do. It's hardly a case of inadequacy as much as it is targeting. Personal gain has no limits. It was once built on the integrity of one's own character and efforts and not the shortcomings of another. Our characters were once built on work ethic, human decency, manners, fortitude, perseverance, humility, and the ability to love and be loved. In 2022, self-image seems to trump all of those virtues. Humans come with a pre-loaded *but* or *so* as acceptable rebuttals to their own apologies and missed obligations. Apologies are no longer apologies but a series of excuses. I will echo the sentiment as it was taught to me in my first attempt at recovery as a 24-year-old; we have two options in this world; the option to be *right* or the option to be *happy*. Being happy simply means removing our imposition of self- will into a situation. The option to be right can be broken down as applying the imposition of our will into a situation, necessarily or unnecessarily. It's as simple as that. The actual accuracy of the situation or outcome of it is irrelevant, as it will never be truly relative in the measure of one's contentment.

Forwarding along as needed and filtering through the feelings stemming from the negative effect of impactful words on our emotions will be an essential tool in getting through this book. Obviously, the title of this book rings hard and deep. It was bone shattering to me when I first heard the word "cunt,", as it was socially deemed unacceptable and cringe-worthy prior to me having lived abroad. The only use of the word I knew of was as a derogatory, sharp noun that served as a synonym to "vagina." Now, having spent most of my adult life with Australians, as opposed to Americans, as my Western form of camaraderie while living and working throughout Southeast Asia, I took a new understanding to the word "cunt." The word simply infers hardship or difficulty, be at a person, place, or thing. My phone or doorknob can be a real cunt, for instance. If you're someone who lets the sound of words impact your feelings in a negative way then it'll be hard for us to establish a literary relationship with each other. My goal is to break down some walls and perceptions that have bogged down our characters in a way that doesn't allow us to move forward with anyone as far as intimate relationships go. By intimate, I mean allowing someone into your authentic soul to know what makes you thrive. On a professional level, I understand how to play the game of advancement and conformity. It doesn't mean I always comply, but it's not that I'm naïve to it. If the risk of negative impact outweighs the employment of my potty-mouth, then I can remove my will from the situation in order to create a better one…. for all concerned parties. I don't let my judgments of another person cloud my efforts towards them, ability to communicate with them, or ability to just love them as a human. Placing an unnecessary judgment on somebody prematurely has a 0% chance of reaching its full potential. Every human has some potential, every human is equal with a different status, and every human deserves the same chance on Earth, not just within the confines of the American borders.

As generations pass, mine included, and the general assessment of ourselves within our defined generational categories gets murky, the opportunity to grow as emotional creatures gets equally as clouded in relation and proportion to the land mass we occupy and the cultures within. Having spent a large portion of my adult life in third world civilizations, the ability to assess my own generation as an American within my group of Gen X's from a distance became clear. There is a clear definition of right and wrong, and a universally accepted understanding of priority within that 'right and wrong' is equally as clear. The passive irascibility of our entitlements here on US soil, magnified by the self-proclaimed reverence of a minute number of our elected leaders, has "wussified" our characters. Liabilities and insurances are essential to protect. There is vengeance over forgiveness, whistleblowing over human-compassion, and uncountable lives valued over others.

We judge character on the job and competence in our intimate relationships, employ others to express themselves emotionally, and then place a mark of adequacy on their emotions with judgement. *Americunts*, generally speaking, assess the question and answer the implicit meaning behind the question; "did you take the dogs out for a walk," I ask my daughter with regularity.

"Well, Brady and Daisy went swimming earlier and Duke just had his dinner." My daughter replies. I stop right there… unsure if she heard the question. I realize at that point that my daughter is presuming culpability in her effortless attempts to be compliant with my wishes and preemptively launches a panel of reasons for her insubordination. The fact is, I don't give a fuck if she took them or not, because I have the ability to take them myself. She will go on and defensively explain the series of tasks she's performed throughout the day as if she's litigating her case on trial. This is regressive in civilized behavior, not progressive. With the dawn of social media almost two decades in our rcarview mirror, we see the patterns with exquisite lucidity. Patterns in human behavior trend toward sexual deviancc, degeneration, and human targeting. We use words like "trolling" and desperately seek new ways to meet other humans in a contrived setting. We essentially doom ourselves before getting to the keyboard. Everybody needs positive affirmation, but self-seeking through social media portals exacerbates a downward spiraling perspective as it relates to our self-assessment and characters as a species. It's a cycle of further devolution. The resounding, proven truth will always be that visceral human contact and connection will never take a backseat to a digital persona and compilation of digital, self-purported laurels.

With the digital age thriving, the medical knowledge of people in general is astoundingly more abundant. The fickle followers of everything web-based have built a wall of 'I told you so' and 'aha' moments. We peruse symptoms, treatments, and remedies. We seek answers for our symptoms, never seeing the less-than-urgent nature of our afflictions. These portals of doctors continue to throw undiagnosed nonsense at us. Many of us are misdiagnosed on the norm, but never, or rarely, does a medical professional look at you and say, "get the fuck outta here, you're fine!"...yet we are and will be. That's not to say there's no merit to medicine, but it's a business like all else. There are big bills to pay with such huge liabilities. The fear of being wrong far outweighs the fear of doing the next right thing, without mention or thought to our actual well-being.

Let's talk about some disorders. Here's a fun fact; there is no human on Earth whose mind works with 100% perfection. That, to the medical profession, opens the gateway to your wallet. People monetize a lack of understanding in others, and shamelessly monetize a problem that could never be solved. Healthcare is a multi-trillion dollar industry, annually, and we are coerced into thinking that there are a multitude of things wrong with us. The undeniable truth is that we're all flawed and that will never change. Physical disorders such as erectile dysfunction now have a complete list of sister, or corresponding disorders that may lead to the physical disconnection. Using just a small example, most of us can attest to having our car go in the garage and getting it out with a whole new set of problems. The same goes for the professional field of medicine. We go in with one problem and come up with six. How else would businesses stay in business? Hospitals aren't governed by our great constitution, they are private entities, self-supported through their own privately funded means. Before I move to Asia in the early 2000s, Misophonia and other disorders were unknown. There is now a growing list of mental disorders, as deemed disorders by the American medical association, that create new avenues of spending into pharmaceuticals, emergency care, and substance abuse. Most disorders have a list of acceptable medicines attributed to alleviating the suffering created by it. The suffering comes in trying to maintain a disorder that has very little to no impact on our daily lives. The thought of being alone in one's own head seems evidence enough to ourselves to seek help. It's not. It's normal to be unsure. It's normal to compare. There's no level of distortion to our dreams, yet we place unnecessary expectations on our cognitive thoughts. Does anyone ever go to the doctor and tell them that they have a disorder only while sleeping? I know I have some pretty sick and serious shit going on in there! The point is that we're always going to need to bring our own minds back to a place of reality being the present moment, because when we let our thoughts get away from us there's no telling what can happen, and there's no telling who will take advantage of that. It's not a sign of weakness or ineptitude and it's definitely not grounds to see a medical professional, it's a sign of normalcy. We have an average life expectancy in the United States around 71 years old from men and 73 years old for women, that's giving us around 30,000 days of life in total. The absolutely asinine thought of giving away any of those days without a pressing need completely withdraws us from our full potential. If we woke up tomorrow and media was broadcasting that we all had to wear special earmuffs to protect ourselves from an ear-borne virus you would normally see a premium spike in the cost of those earmuffs over 1000%, but you would see complete anarchy and blind aggression towards those not wearing your earmuffs. Yeah, there's some humor attached to this, but it's a little bit of truth that makes things funny.

The title of this book, without question, has caused some negative ripples throughout many people's code of acceptable conduct and vocabulary. That's the undeniable truth, but it's also undeniable that it's how you let words affect you. Your feelings will never affect my day if I don't let them. The world began to take a downward turn when feelings began to overrule facts. Now that I've made my disclaimer let me also be clear that I am in no way above or beyond being called an *Americunt*. I created the name and exemplified the qualities of one for so long. I too suffer from expectations. I too suffer from the cultural rigmarole, unnecessary as it is, of daily life. I too suffer from being an *Americunt*, at times, when I place my feelings above another's and believe them to be valid and justified, I have abandoned my own humanity. Anything more than a human being put on earth to be of service to another human being is irrelevant, to me…now. As a recovered drug addict, I place a high mark on self-assessment and integrity, self and social mindfulness. Whatever assets I've been given are nothing to be self-peddled and flaunted, but put to service and bartered for inadequacies, in total vulnerability. Self-seeking is a symptom of technology and disconnection. They are "new-age" issues. They (our given assets and virtues) weren't meant for professional or social advancements. As a Darwinist and evolutionist I firmly believe in the adaptation of our species, but I don't agree with the over civilization our species seems to think it's required to employ. Natural selection was never meant to include targeting are on species for self-gain. In a world where religion bears little-to-no relevance in our daily lives, it seems that we instinctively place the highest mark of evolution on ourselves. I was told in third grade that if Komodo dragons could swim a little farther we wouldn't be the most evolved species on Earth. I find that hard to believe, but I'm starting to think it might make things pretty interesting. Obviously having had thousands of years to advance our own technologies, self-will, and intellect, Komodo dragons would have a slim-to-none chance of survival in our modern day world, at this point. We beat them to the punch, thankfully. I'm still rooting for them, however. There's no coincidence that our connection to Earth and nature provide us with a sense of gratitude. How many of us have friends that take excursions into exotic or beautiful places and come back with an ephemeral sense of gratitude? Short-lived, albeit, but this just proves my point. It defines the differences in being right and being happy, and being thrusted into a modern age of indifference and ruthlessness it brings our souls back to an organic place of naturalism. Funny thing about being a drug addict and alcoholic is the education provided by the sick and suffering, to the sick and suffering. It's an education that far outweighs anything you'll find in a classroom, but it helps us reengage ourselves to ourselves. It helps us remember what we actually like and enjoy, not whatever form of reality our social environments dictate we comply with and live forth.

Biologically and before the five theories of evolution, humans started out as pack-animals. We've shifted into isolation and reclusiveness. Even the least ardent, needy followers are resolute in their own ways. Advice is carelessly thrown out to others when it's advice we would never take ourselves! Humans will forever go on with the ability to oppose their self-will, without fear of consequence. The truth of evolution is that we are the only species that knows we're going to die, and this fact alone propels us to indecency, self-imposed deadlines, targeting, and ruthlessness. If we were all unaware of this fact, life would be resolute to servitude and building connections. There would be no rat-race, timeframes, socially acceptable stages of life, or daily structure, even. Remove the rapidly expiring clock and watch haste and impulse dissipate. Leapfrogging our brothers and sisters by distasteful and deplorable means would be irrelevant because we would have no concept of time, as it would be acceptable ignorance for lack of a better understanding.

Once upon a time I was spearheading the final stretch of a five-star resort opening on a remote island in Thailand. What I didn't know is that I was given the job because I was expected to fail. The owner obviously didn't know who I was, but knew only of my earnestness to be part of his resort. It was a five-star paradise in Ko Phangan, Thailand. I arrived in late October during rainy season to a resort that was 30% complete in construction after three years and had accepted bookings the previous year. The bookings were set to start on December 26, 2011. Up to this point in time I had served only as an executive chef for a five-star property and never as a general manager. I thought it a bit peculiar at the time that I was given the role of general manager, but my self-manage integrity on a professional level is something that can't be challenged. Challenged maybe, ruined never! With six weeks to go there was an urgent need to move faster, work longer, do more, talk less, and prioritize only the needs of the initial bookings. I arrived on the island with my girlfriend in tow. We set out from the moment we got there with the engineering team that had been in place for three years… to jumpstart a fire under their asses, which you can bet was hugely protested on all levels. It was a win-win for the owner. If the resort opened in time he could point to the fact that he employed me with the assurance that it would be open, and once I had gotten it open he would be a hero to his guests.

Had I failed, I would have made a perfect scapegoat. The success of another person has never consumed a cubic shred of space in my mind. I set out to do the job I was meant to do….that was opening on the twenty-sixth of December to rave reviews on *TripAdvisor.* Five stars in our first thirteen bookings, an article on the *Condé Nast Traveler,* and the 31st ranking in the world, according to the *New York Times,* as far as world travel destinations were concerned in 2012.

The impossibility of the job became clear from the onset, so I took whatever means necessary. I employed casual Burmese labor working without work visas for a quarter of what the Thai workers were working for in order to open the resort. I gave jobs to people that didn't have them and were in need. I helped families put food on their tables and clothes on the children's packs. We ate as a family…Americans, Thais, and Burmese. We did laundry together and fished the shores for crab together on nights when we didn't have enough food to eat. We lived in unfinished shelters with the promise that once the villas were finished they would be our homes. It was the most connected I had ever felt with any group of humans, and the materialization of their appreciation came in their efforts, not their words. Not a person on that island had a vested interest in the success of the hotel nor did they have any reason to stay other than the internal desire to be congruent with their words. They went beyond intentions in about the normal size of human effort for the greater good. We were all part of that resort, but Western culture would grow envious and discontent with our success. The owner of that resort… ultimately, working with the Thai mafia, set out to assassinate me in order to reclaim his place as primal leader. My staff, bogged in a salary of less than four dollars per day, gathered up all of their financial resource in in order to pay an assassin to take a short trip around the block in order to buy me some time to get off the island. This is what we were meant to be. Brothers and sisters working together for the greater good against all else. Recognizing the efforts in love above and beyond the call of normal duty and acting out accordingly is our rightful path of evolution.

The owner of that resort, naïvely thinking that his paycheck controlled the situation, was far outnumbered and far out-classed. After three months of consistent success, repeat bookings, five-star reviews, and joyful living, the disdain for my alpha-male-ness was so upsetting to the owner that my reward was death. This doesn't shake my opinion of people as I have seen and accepted that evil comes in all forms, but the basic gist of this is to understand what your intentions are, as it is something that I ardently seek to understand in myself. It's how I base my actions. It's not whether or not someone will understand my actual intentions or motives, but it's the fact that I understand that in myself that shapes my integrity. Knowing yourself is the greatest gift you can give to the world, and yourself. Modern day Robin Hood aims at caddy behaviors, indignant tones, and general indifference of the ignorantly rich and self-seeking human missiles and redirects it back to those whose integrity and sweat ethic has not wavered not merited them the gifts of life they've earned.

Thinking back to the words I used that some *Americunts* find to be marks of weakness, I purposely left out the most important one. The reason being, it's one that can't ever be grouped, and is glaringly misunderstood by Western cultures. Most Asian cultures do not have a word for it, but it's inherently understood in their actions. We can amazingly assign a directory of like terms and words without ever fully understanding what they mean to us, as individuals. . "Vulnerability." Vulnerability is what makes us human to other humans. It's what sets us apart from any other species on the planet. Knowingly being vulnerable towards another human outside of the parameters of an intimate relationship is the most misunderstood aspect of our existence. It is the greatest and most attractive virtue we can see another person's soul, and is quickly becoming the rarest human quality. It's viewed as an area weakness and an opportunity for self-advancement, professionally and intimately. It's the most valuable resource we can be given from another person, yet Western culture places a negative feeling on the sound of the word alone, and dismisses the notion that it applies to them. Devolution is harbored in the irrefutable fact that our social tendencies are mass produced and ubiquitously ineffective. To put in layman's terms, if 99% of the population would quit catering to the 1% of the population that gets offended by everything, then evolution would progress as normal. Normal, you may think it's an over-expectation. Normal to me just means a series of things that define my life as a continuous chain of events that align me with my own soul.

It's an alignment that's necessary in all of us. A few examples of things that help me understand my internal sense of align lament with my own soul are the most mundane of life's obligations or luxuries, but ones I find are in correlation to my own personal successes. They are as follows: having paper towels, having cups to drink out of, having a mailbox that's not stuffed with mail and un-emptied, having more than a negative number on my bank statement, texting with my parents once a week, waking up without every centrifugal force weighed against me, and not having a parade of scantily clad young women appearing in my daily news feed on social media. These are small things, but lifesaving to me. To others, it's much more advanced, but for a guy like me…. the simple things prove my place in the world as a human being contributing to a species. The simplest things come very unnaturally to me, but I don't need to celebrate it. It's normal fucking shit.

2 | Commonly Unique

Humanity

hu·man·i·ty

/(h)yooˈmanədē/

Noun:

the human race; human beings collectively. Ex:"appalling crimes against humanity"

FULL DEFINITION

Similar: humankind, the human race, the human species, mankind, man, people, mortals, Homo-sapiens.

Opposite: the animal kingdom - *based on what, I ask? Are we not animals? I find this particularly intriguing. We, in our own literature, place our existence above all else. This is the start of hubris.*

I Am…..One In 8 Billion

The more obvious to me it becomes that I have less than a clue as to how the fuck we all got here and what we're all doing here, the more content I seem to be. Here as in Earth, that is. I'd like to think, at this stage of the game, it's a sign of maturity and acceptance that I'm not claiming to have it all figured out. Up until recently I was pretty sure I either did, or I could convince you that I did. I guess that's where 'mansplaining' came from. Dipshits such as my younger self-paving the way for generations to come by verbally gaslighting and emotionally highjacking every relationship I ever had. Whatever the reason, I, like most honest people, naturally assume that everyone else has it figured out while I am the proverbial headless chicken. Nonetheless, as a father and loved human, I am responsible and dedicated to everyone that can see or find a redeemable quality in me. See, I'm also a raging alcoholic and drug addict, and that is something that will never go away. The family and friends that are still around today, and have seen me through the gates of hell and out the ass end, and are still with me by choice, are the ones I speak of. Not that I'm holding anyone captive against their will. I stopped doing that. Not physically, I mean, emotionally. I would manipulate everyone I knew until they conformed with my will. I guess that made them my emotional prisoner, at one point in time. Without these people an addict has no chance of connection or redemption. It's an irrefutable testament to their character to have dealt with me at my worst and still be there for me today. It offers me the opportunity for exoneration for my unfathomable poor acts of character to someone willing to see beyond the control the drugs have, and a true friend that sticks up for you, to you, with you. Without these people we addicts, myself included, would be essentially the same as a dog chasing its tail around in circles...a soul without purpose. A broken mind. No way to break the cycle. It is surely impossible to choose my family or their relation to me and their subsequent involvement in my youth, but it wasn't impossible to choose how I let my family impact my life today. I am the one in the bloodline-d group that my family pacifies and nods to, the 'the black sheep', for lack of a more clever title. I'm the 50/50 guy...maybe 60/40. No one actually expects much from me thanks to years of me fighting off the drug addicted version of myself. People take time to see you again. It also depends on who's running the show upstairs, myself or the other guy, my addicted self. Sometimes it's epic and sometimes it's epic collapse. Knowing this fact, it can only be through the efforts of others to search hard and long in the pit of my soul and character to find a redeeming quality that I have anyone left in my life. I am essentially an infinite cycle of poor decisions. Otherwise, I would have to call into question the decision making ability of everybody that I love, and that would essentially being the pot calling the kettle black. I've also come to accept, by now, my remarkably small rate of success I have achieved over forty two years in making good decisions. It's my superpower. Oh, I should also tell you that I don't really read books. I forged every summer reading that I ever had and could probably count all the books I read with what fingers I've got left that still go up. I don't have much worldly knowledge or financial acumen. All I have are my memories from the streets I've walked in the places I've been. The rest of my knowledge in this world comes from movies, so before you get too far along, just know who you're dealing with. You're dealing with a piece of white garbage, in the flesh. I am one of those people that would, in the past, measure his worth by his intentions. Ignorant, indignant, and indifferent. That is usually me...

With 8 billion beating hearts all competing for the same level of uniqueness around the globe it becomes incessantly exhausting trying to keep up with whatever it is we're all trying to keep up with. We all have our agendas, visions, and dreams. We all have a right to breathe. I think what most people misunderstand is the actual truth that breathing is the basic end of your rights as a human being. Being an American and having had the privilege and opportunity to spend a large portion of my adult life in Third World civilizations, I've come to realize that "terminal uniqueness" is more a Western problem than a global problem, but the problem remains. I used to think I was blessed to have the opportunity to have seen and experience life in Third World countries. Now, I feel more fortunate living in them. The problem isn't spread through one generation, although millennials often get the bad rap. It's spread through advancements in technology that ultimately doom us as humans. Our obligations to stay connected as emotional beings are in jeopardy through technology. Don't get me wrong… I love my iPhone and every custom fit nuance I can fit into my life in order to ease the speed of life we've created, but ultimately, I, like most enjoy simplicity. Western cultures inherently feel the need to be better than, quicker than, stronger than, more mindful, aware, intuitive, and holistically pure. If the world were built on intentions…there is no doubt it would be a perfect place, or at least, near perfect. As a devout fan of real life criminal documentaries, it's tough to tie a bow on that one.

My issue is specifically with the culture I was born into, American culture. It's been widely understood, written, documented, studied etc. for years, the horrific global impact caused by Americans not minding their own business. The preach and the practice are so far apart, yet, we continuously propel and force our democracies into parts of the world that just don't accept it. We back human beings that are deplorable in character, and expect our followers to conform. The single-handed destruction of Afghanistan and the Philippines in the last half century have gone completely unacknowledged…at least by the "lay" people. By this, I mean, regular every day Americans, focused always on the micro and never on the macro, who are always living for the most beneficial moment in their lives, and not for the environment they cohabitate. Any implicit negativity towards an American is immediately refuted and justified. I haven't had a reasonable conversation with an American in quite some time. There is no longer an outlook towards creating a better world for generations to come, as we're fixated on our current situation in the world. I would be remiss if I did not share my last dialogue; a conversation with a clerk at the Mobile station I frequent. The discussion centered on '*things I miss that were replaced by technology*'. Nostalgic, but why does it have to be? Why can't people maintain their connections just because society moves faster around them? It's the fear of being left behind…fearful having of been completely irrelevant and unable to catch up. It's the fear of a tainted legacy, and It's our peers that drive this fear into us. Just as the generation before mine was finally grasping the concept of computers, without the Internet, along came the World Wide Web and forced a generation to get back to school and into the classrooms. I can remember about 20 years ago, the running theme with Baby Boomers was the refusal, emphatically, of the Internet. If the Internet was a person, he or she would've been stoned at the proverbial gates and denied entry. I would lean in the direction of the Internet being female, because of its level of complication! Women have tendency to complicate just about anything. I'd say she's an alcoholic, too!

Generation X down to the Baby Boomers genuinely pine for human connection to be part of our world again. Polaroids, postcards, Christmas cards, car mechanics, phone books, flashlights, motor-less couriers, board games, 'mall-ratting', and even handshakes are things of the past. We may as well just adopt the ancient greeting of the *wai,* the touch-less salutations of our ancient Asian ancestors. Fist bumps are not cool, by the way. If you're a fist bump dude, you're not my guy. Our 'comfort zones' have shrunk to immediate needs and human deflection only

Moving on…I'd like to break that eight billion number down a little bit and really focus both of our attentions to a failing project. That project happens to be one that I am a product of; the modern American lifestyle. A snowballing culture of soulless robots driven by technology. As the results shown through media and 90's parenting trends, compounded with the furious rate of technological advancements that outweigh the normal person's rate of capture and challenges the average capacity, the grand picture is one of failing ethics, social disconnection, and character erosion. "It's pretty hard to be a person" is becoming the modern American view. "It's not my job, my problem, or my concern" are the new acceptable forms of plausible excuse. Justification is premeditated and ignorance is presumed. It's preferred to be contentious than helpful…to our own species. Call center reps are now supplied with exit dialogue for irate guests that have been stuck, helpless in their attempt at resolving whatever arbitrary fact of their life has become so irritating yet unable to circumvent any longer. Consumers hide sheepishly behind a microphone or screen and berate another human in order to appease their self-developed mental entitlement to whatever it is they're on about. We use each other to build ourselves up. How many times have you heard exaggeration of a simple truth from Americans mouth? Always, immediately, never, etc. These are words of exaggeration, and we've let them become us. The circular borders of our nation have steepened, and it's a metaphorically heartless, unapologetic, and hurtful race to the top. I'm hardly a hippie, however, contrary to popular belief, the notion of kindness and peace doesn't reside exclusively in the soul of a hippie. It resides in the tiny, microscopic realm in our minds that allows humility and compassion and vulnerability into our lives. Three words I would berate you for muttering in my polluted, addicted mind; but, the three words that set me free.

The last thing any serene, calm mind takes solace in is its own acknowledgement to defeat in allowing itself to be rented out by the day to day idiosyncrasies of the aforementioned self-seeking. Simply put, the enjoyment my hardships seemingly bring to most Americans is widely accepted, encouraged, and nauseating, at times. I'm not one for presuming without merit, but there isn't a place where pure evil is more evidently subtle than in the rejoiced bellow of a store clerk regarding a missing face mask on a customer or a call rep citing an irreversible small print policy as their reasons for refusing a refund. Indifference where a single, small action can change another's path is accepted as we justify our dismissal in the potential risk and inconvenience it may cause us. There is nothing more gratifying to my American cohorts than celebrating and flexing one's own perceived authority into another's unforeseen obstacle.

Expectations. Expectations are unnecessary, ever. They are the root of self-intoxication. After having lived in Southeast Asian cultures (Thailand, Vietnam, Bali, Singapore, and the Philippines) for so long, I am genuinely embarrassed at so many unnecessary burdens Americans carry, I covet the simple life. Every American is *liking* to go faster while the only thing that interests me is slowing down. Slowing down our bruised ego and defensiveness. Slowing down our reactions to a response. Slowing down our need for verbal praise and slowing down the rights we think we have. Slowing down our minds to be able to contribute, authentically, and stop extracting what we can. Slowing down enough to be gentle, that is the how, why, and where my allegiances to my rightful birth soil got clouded. It isn't the tech, or the unfathomable advances in evolution, it's the regression in human compassion and general kindness. It's the acceptable levels of human dismissal. It's the overwhelming majority in *I don't give a fuck.* I'm hardly a power of example, but when push comes to shove I'm definitely a guy that you want in your corner, and a human that certainly doesn't need a valid reason, empty time slot, or expected return on my investment for helping another person.

The first of two occurrences that needed to take place to flatten the curve of my own ignorance was to teach myself to accept everything I heard and that I'll hear…relative to me, or you, or not. As paradoxically insane as that sounds, and sounded then, I tried it. Why not? Who am I to say otherwise? Even if I know

better, remember …I have the opportunity to be *right* or *happy*.
Happiness comes from non-action. Happiness comes from me
not self-seeking. I think less, I'm happier. I do more without
expectations, I'm happier. I impose my will into any situation,
I'm left to deal with the ripples of the emotions I summon. The
point is, it's ultimately irrelevant to me. I can try a million
invalid excuses as to why I think it's my business, but it's not. It
wouldn't affect a day of my life. Calling other people's words
into question, while knowing otherwise, is now offensive,
anyway, and, like I said, none of my business. You can't coax an
American to learn on your watch, regardless! Time and effort
outweigh any amount of money and surface appeal. I feel that. I
believe everyone has something to offer of benefit, but knowing
what that is gets confusing. I, unlike most, have zero interest in
money. I'm interested in having some, but I'm not willing to do
what most people seem willing to do to get it. I need it to fulfill
my daily vision. Tomorrow, I will need some more to fulfill that

vision. I dream big, but vision realistically. I try everything. Why not? In the long and short of it, there isn't an iota of attraction in conformity to me. It's not that I was 'born a rebel' or fell off somewhere along the way, I just enjoy challenges, hardships, and risks. I enjoy challenging myself as a person in the most mundane layers of my life and moments within. I enjoy challenging my daughter, too. Fuck, I challenge just about everyone and everything I know... If it's not going to kill me (or you), then I don't see any harm in taking a shot at it. I've moved countries overnight and sold all my worldly possessions on many occasions so I could get there. I've lived as close to the moment when I've been sober enough to be…in order to be the truest version of myself I can be. I takes practice, and practice is something I enjoy. I don't mind driving around the country, devoting my day to random people, leaving a job for another one, avoiding taxes, running out of money with regularity, impulsive spending on completely unnecessary and ephemeral treasures, adopting any live animal that needs my help, or just experiencing failure on my terms. I'm told through Alcoholics Anonymous that these are misplaced, addictive behaviors. I'm not one to disagree when I don't know the answer, but it's not ruining my life the way methamphetamines did.

I personally value making my own uninterrupted mistakes. Time after time. I fucking love it. Life would be unbearably boring and monotonous without them. You'll have to bring something of equal or greater trade value in order to get me off that sort of fun. I am, actually, elated at the opportunity to make more mistakes and see how it goes. Insert shrugging dude emoji. I guess when I say "mistakes" I mean American unobtrusiveness. I realize, just as everyone else does, that the answers are in the phone, but here's my example. It is uncannily similar to the character played by Robin Williams in *Good Will Hunting* when he sits Matt Damon's character down for a life lesson about experience, noting his travels and losses and triumphs as they pertained to the Vietnam War and the view from the ground of the Sisteen Chapel. Matt Damon's character, Will, had all the knowledge in the world, but his experience rendered that knowledge useless outside the pages of the book he was citing as his knowledge. The psychologist Williams played spoke from the knowledge his own eyes gave him. It's the life we live, day to day, that measure our internal sense of gratitude and fulfillment.

See, recently I decided to expand my immediate family by adopting four goats.

While I think they're amazing creatures, I've never experience owning them, nor did I research the fundamentals of goat ownership. I show up for life every day, unexcused and unwaveringly persistent in knowing what I'm doing and measuring the output of my efforts…perpetually seeking the bounty my practice provides. I didn't need to research the answers to have a perfect "goat adoption", I wanted to fail in areas and be present as a compassionate soul, present and willing to do whatever necessary and fail along the way. It's the path we take that brings the most reward, not the ease in execution.

The second occurrence, and final step to my condensed 12-step, instant-gratification shortcut, that needs to take place is maintaining my newfound connection by training my brain as if I had a major brain injury and slow life to a level of stagnancy. My poorest character is noticeably one that speaks over anyone, knows everything about everything, and can't honestly recall a moment of my life where the thought "I was wrong," were the first words in my reactive soul. They are my most glaring defects of character. Stagnant minds are a blessing for an addict in recovery, as I am, and always will be. To the members of Alcoholics Anonymous, this is known as the 10th, 11th, and 12th step. To a group of aspiring members who pride themselves on a less-complicated approach to life, I find 12 steps to be a little over the top and suppressive. Deflating, even. How can I follow through with twelve of anything when, in the height of my addiction, execution of a single intention was difficult.

Spreading the message to other alcoholics and addicts while maintaining our connection to our newfound life in sobriety; these are the principles and values taught through these three steps. The principles of these three steps are only achieved once members are healed enough through recovery to have made our amends, and subsequently turned our lives over to the care of a higher power, as we understand him. In all seriousness, morale compromising repetition is the path out. Repetitiously and without fail. I can mouth the words to getting out of my comfort zone every morning, or when moments arise, and head straight for it. Accepting that some moments fail, but those won't stop me is my way out. Theoretically elementary, yet consistently attainable by only the spirituality reverent.

Soundness and simplicity in my soul is waking up and reminding myself to nod my head often to ease my instinctual right to impose my will into the irrelevant minutia of anything I hear. Not because I am restraining myself from hearing myself speak, or being a better, well rounded person, but because I am recognizing that my words are not always necessary, or helpful. I recognize the relevance of my place in the room and practice non-action as much as possible. Something I was naively obliviously nescient about. I remind myself that it doesn't matter one fucking bit who knows what I know if it doesn't help their situation. I offer less advice on things I have basic knowledge of and place an accurate word on my knowledge of it. I had to train myself to not be obnoxious. Imagine that. I leave my situation in any part of the day without regret or a mental balancing act of untruths that may resurface. I am never one hundred percent compliant on that one, however. I tell people the worst things first. I would hate anyone **not** knowing the worst thing about me in America. They are all dealbreakers to those with perceptual boundaries, and I hate wasting time on people.

These forms of practiced and learned acceptance are exactly that, and they are my authenticity. They are all masked by one simple fuck up, but the fear of monotony and soul crushing boredom scare me way more. My biggest fear is being one of those people that digitally plan everything, physically do nothing, and firmly believe they are going about it all the right way. I am grateful this wasn't the card I pulled. Furthermore, I'd love to wake up and have full faith and experience in myself as being a naturally better person than I am, but that would be me lying to me. The closet skeletons accrue hurriedly when drugs call the shots. They make me an undesirable human on all levels. If we are ultimately meant to be ruled and controlled, geographically, then we should take preventative measures to make the world a truly better place. That means our leaders need to do better jobs, and minimize our voices. Let the mental aptitude of a few govern the masses. If only the scientists and doctors could join forces and create a device that made you shit your pants every time you had a self-seeking or self-loathing moment, that would help me stop banging my head against the wall dealing with humans, Americans mostly. It would help forc acceptance. It's a bit raunchy, indeed, but I try not to take EVERYTHING as serious as my countrymen do. It's not to say I feel 100% accurate with my opinions, because they are subjective, but the balance of democratic structure has been compromised.

The path I originally chose was self-seeking, and drugs. The path I seek and aspire towards today is healthy connection and redemption. I feel slightly more "healed" than yesterday, and it's almost always contingent upon my level of reflection, patience, and acceptance. These are all virtues I lack, but I enjoy the practice, because I respect how difficult it is for me, personally. My first inclination was to talk a great game, let everyone know how fucking cool I am. That was my game. I try to stick to only what's relevant as I get older, another sign of maturity. Finally, I've come to realize that anything extra than what's asked or needed is self-seeking and manipulative. It's me pumping my tires. It took me a long time to accept this. I, like most, can drum up a valid excuse for anything. I am me, and I can be ok with being me today. I can recognize my down days; be it lack of motivation or structure or fucks left to give, I let it be me, and I make sure "me" isn't an increasingly toxic environment, and I sort out the best version of happiness from there. That's if I remind my crazy head to; *be nice, listen, shut up, let them speak, don't be so fucking annoying, holy fucking horse shit this guy won't shut the fuck up, but he seems nice so let's not rip his life apart kinda day, get a grip, see what the fuck am I on about, say sorry and stop acting like a bitch, and look people in the eye and don't talk like an uppity douchebag.* The day I have all those internal conversations with myself, the days go much more smoothly. The days I wake up thinking I'm pissing excellence are the days I wish I had back. I need to perpetually be small. The minute I infect anything; a situation, an object, or a person with my unnecessary, misguided will, I am walloped back into flesh and mistakes. My sobriety may or may not depend on that one. I've never been much for drama, so it's not the fighting or home wrecking drugs produce, but the displacement from the homes they cause. Most of my arrests happened at times I should have been home and caused my own displacement. I always attributed it to shit luck until I got a clue and put the meth pipe down. I make less mistakes through non action. That is where the paradox of -surrendering to be free- holds truth. There is an additional step to maintaining the connection that one's ultimate surrender provokes, but they never mention that. Fuck it up enough and you'll figure it out. I did, and I'm a professional at fucking shit up. I make it a habit, without voluntarily giving it thought, to taking the most risky and dangerous way to do just about anything. I think this is a guy thing...yeah, it is. I'm no different. As long as there is less than a 10% chance of death, by my omniscient estimate, I will do just about anything.

Add into that, my wife Tammy, whom I choose to spend every and any moment with is a professional at complicating shit... so we get very little headway made at any point in any day, but we know through our own history together how not to take away from each other. We build each other up in their vision, not our own. That is the presence of pure, unconditional love. Speaking of pure love; as my better half and only willing editor to my writing scans my new manuscript, she scoffs at the notion above where I proclaimed to have "trained myself to not be obnoxious", and she finds irony in her judgement, but offers a first-hand testimonial and cautions my reader's acceptance of the purported completion of my less obnoxious self. I find irony in this as well, but not as much irony as I found in her making my literal point. My literary aim manifested. Judgement is unavoidable, but what we let it do to us is where the rubber meets the road. Insert wink emoji replied with puke emoji followed by eye roll emoji followed by heart emoji. No words, an indescribable omniscience to each other's energy, and never having to worry about my infuriating intensity smoldering the authenticity of "us." There honestly should be a lifetime achievement award for anyone subjecting themselves to any considerable amount of time with me, but she makes it look effortless. Desirable, even.

Several parts of my character make it extremely difficult to hold certain jobs. Anything that can confine me to four walls, four specific walls, and you can pretty much start my unemployment claim. I have a hard time with any situation that requires me to work with the person that I report to, or just spend more than a good portion of my day around authority. I've been fortunate to have been able to work autonomously throughout my career, otherwise, I probably would be selling my ass to meth-heads at the gay bars in Boston. That actually has been the most lucrative offer yet. I just really want to keep my ass more virgin than meth would like.

Outside of being a chef, there's nothing else on Earth I would think would satisfy me more than that. For some reason, when I'm in a kitchen anywhere, for that matter, I have a sense of comfort that other rooms or venues could never match. My immediate love was restaurant and the lifestyle the industry created. My first love is now food and the study of it. I specialize in royal Thai cuisine after having lived most of my time abroad in Thailand. I find Thai cuisine the most balanced in the world, as each dish aspires to touch all four parts of the tongue. Culinary school brought me from the crack streets of Chinatown, Boston, to a life I never dreamed possible. It took me to celebrity status in Thailand, and it took me around the world. Unfortunately, drumroll please...... It also took me to my next new love. Methamphetamines.

Unlike most chefs, I don't blame my mistakes and financial hardships on my career choice. There are two other professions

I could envision myself showing up to every day and putting in a good day's work, besides mindless obligatory labor.

The only other thing I think I would want to be, in this world, is a veterinarian. Outside of helping maladjusted, addicted humans and cooking like a motherfucker, my other passion is my animals. It, they, just fascinate me to no end. I currently have four goats, five bunnies, six cats, five dogs, a tortoise, a hedgehog, and three sugar gliders. Yep, I'll talk about that much more as we go on, but know my kingdom's gates will never slam shut. I sit and talk and self-medicate through their vulnerability. It keeps me small. There's a beautiful existence to be earned with shit covered boots and a warm soul.

So, I basically talk about Evelyn, my daughter and only child, and animals… and anything else is your stuff. I find happiness in my time with them watching them warm to other species.

Watching the comfort they have in me, knowing I don't separate our differences, but employ them to help the balance of our lives together. Appreciating and recognizing the amount of effort I put into them reminds me of my purpose…Evelyn, then them. It doesn't take much for me. They are mine which means their lives, their safety, and their happiness are my responsibility. That's where my happiness comes from, so it's not something anyone could judge. It's pure.

My situation in life is a bit unique in that my daughter is a dual citizen of the United States and Thailand and was born in the Philippines, where her birth records are held. We have had quite the ride, and it isn't over yet! My first time sitting and typing in my notes section of my iPhone, I came out with a book. Approximately 62,000 words later I sent it to a publisher and ended up enjoying sharing my story so much that I am back here, with you.…typing. If you haven't read *The Duke of*

Doucheville, I'll catch you up. My life took an epic turn from quasi celebrity in Thailand while living in exotic places to a homeless, poor, meth-head in Bangkok while having a child and desperately trying to stay in her life, while conquering two separate abductions by her mother. Phew.

Evelyn and I are pretty close to put it gently. She's my twice abducted, half Thai daughter. She's the best version of anything that could ever come from me. It's mind blowing. She is the most connected human to my soul the universe could produce. The most connected two people can be, I would think. There is nothing physically or mentally that separates her from any other child on earth. She's just mine, and I wouldn't know what a complete existence felt like had I not had her.

Most parents I know feel the same way I do, so don't think I'm pumping my own tires here. I'm just trying to transcend the feelings I have onto digital paper. I'm not perfect. I struggled a lot. I relapsed on crystal meth and played the coward card again and again. I'm currently on a great life streak emptying my heart into writing while my communication and contact with Evelyn has been cruelly, and inhumanely obstructed and forbidden. Evelyn's mother has something mentally wrong with her. I'm sure most scorned parents will fling similar accusations, but there is merit to my claim. She has obviously gone medically undiagnosed and completely under the radar seeing as I literally sent my daughter flying across the world into a real-life nightmare, being smothered and abducted without warning, days before 5th grade in Boston was set to commence, by a parent without the capability of sending Evelyn to a school. Meanwhile, after her two years in Boston with me... she wrapped up fourth grade by winning the class spelling be and getting a lead in a drama club play. It was the best two minutes and fifty-two seconds of dramatic interpretation in the history of mankind. She played The Gingerbread Man. Okay…it was just cool to be there. Between the guy I became while addicted and the struggles in balancing life as a full time, single father, I take huge pride in being present for everything. Everything Evelyn related, at least. I know Evelyn is safe today as I get notifications for every app she installs through her google play store, but I can't find a portal to get a conversation with her. I hid an iPhone in her Christmas gifts and got a timid, one-and-a-half-minute phone call with her a few weeks ago, but that has been it, as far as us being able to contact each other, since I left Bangkok, while Evelyn's AirTag was traveling north near Laos. Weird situation and story, I get it. Anyway, life has brought acceptance through sobriety and contentment. I'm focusing on everything I've been through and, more so, the things yet to come. I'm writing, obviously. It's a new hobby, but one that I'm enjoying. I get this happiness from simply doing my best with the moment I'm in, giving it my actual attention and best attitude, constantly shoving the cynic in me to the floor and practicing restraint. Choosing to be *happy* over *right*. This takes daily practice and is rarely ever a daily check mark for an addict.

Remembering the year prior when Evelyn was glued to me every minute; I sit and listen to Evelyn's perceived logic behind the Eddie Money song "Take me home tonight," being that the singer is a homeless man pleading with a passerby to get him out of the cold for the night, I am reminded of the best version of myself. That version of me, by now, has been beaten into submission by decades of drug abuse…meth abuse. I was an ugly person for a long time. Physically, I have been given a free pass, but I 'uglied' up my insides by pussying out to the voice in my head, ad nauseam, and self-medicated the right to my own uniqueness for over 25 years with countless narcotics. I was entitled to all the feelings American doctors told me were ok. I was impenetrable in my stance…anyone who's encouraged by a medical professional would be. At what point do we rely on evolution and adaptation to take its course? When do we start to challenge the most powerful single thing on the planet; the human brain? I would have preferred the tough love method, but the US drug epidemic set liabilities for professionals, and liabilities are scary. At what point do we stop doing things reactively to feelings and revert back to common logic and the general benefit of all mankind? The human mind is widely considered the greatest invention/creation of all time, but challenging its limits have become challenging in itself. The slightest risk of a step backwards to make up ground over the long haul has quietly become a non-option.

Emotionally, I am a 17-year-old. That is how many years of my life have been spent clean, including adolescence and infancy. Noticeably fewer than the ones spent high. I, myself, will caution you as to what you believe from me and what you decide to let go. I contradict my own integrity with regularity, with justification. I am still a steep climb in character to the person I want to be. Some days I'm not sure where to start. There is, however, something I can say that most in my shoes cannot; I have survived and recovered enough. I have remembered the epic highs and melancholic, self-induced hardships. I have captured the misplaced feelings of my addicted, toxic self.

The irony rests in my inabilities to articulate a solution in words that don't have a harsh tone while inspiring self-love. Self-love is the catalyst for any inner evolution. My personal opinions, as useless as they are, have a massive misinterpretation of what *Americunts* believe is "self-love," but should I manage to remove the self-seeking and focus, without needing to please everyone on what my strengths in benevolence are, then I will have found my way. It won't be from anything that has to do with claiming respect, racial equalities, or just the right to be right..... it comes

from service, and that is life's great paradox.

3 | The Other Guy

hu·bris

/ˈ(h)yoobrəs/

noun: excessive pride or self-confidence.

FULL DEFINITION.

Similar: arrogance, conceit, conceitedness, haughtiness, pride, vanity, self-importance, self-conceit, pomposity, superciliousness, feeling of superiority, hauteur, uppitiness, big-headedness

Opposite: modesty

Before we get any further into our literary relationship, there are a few more facts you may have to come to terms with before we get to the point of no return. I understand how loosely I use the phrase "the other guy," and seemingly deflect my accountability in life onto him. That is the furthest thing from reality, as he is part of me, and represents everything I don't want to be. His presence is my authentic soul's cry out for help, and an obvious sign of a weakened character, more penetrable than Swiss cheese.

The best way, or at least a feeble attempt to describe the power of addiction and relapse to those that aren't afflicted is this; when we feel and accept that we are not the physical specimen we once envisioned… we make a decision that it's time to fix our physical bodies and devote time well spent at the gym, it starts with the idea that it's beneficial to go as a general concept. The first day, and maybe the next few to come are a battle. I, personally have sat in the parking lot at the gym for extensive periods convincing myself of the benefits of walking through the door. It's ultimately our own understanding that our physical shape needs work because it doesn't match the vision we have in ourselves. As time goes on, we start to see a physical change… others see it, as well. They let us know, and it carries us at times through the good, bad, and indifferent. For about six to nine months we see gradual progress, never slowing down and growing more confident by the day. After a while, our bodies and progress plateau and we stop seeing as much physical change in ourselves, thus creating the internal struggle of whether it's worth maintaining our time spent at the gym. We feel we've 'earned' that off day and we know we have. We have no defense for our reward because it's justifiable…at least, to us. Imagine the contrary being a made up fantasy that our mind manufacturers stemming from the euphoric sensation and release our bodies experienced while high? See, the argumentative stance in that analogy is that our bodies don't become a polluted morass from that time away from the gym. Our thoughts don't turn to self-seeking and destructive behaviors from that time away from the gym. Our bodies don't become physically dependent on that day off, because that's all it takes is just one day for addicts. That's why I write. I write this nonsense to spread the message of how I came to be clean and hopefully inspire even one human soul to see the less painful path, one of arduous maintenance and ultimate redemption. I call it nonsense…it is. It's only not nonsense if my words help even one person. That's what we addicts do this for.

He, "the other guy," represents the totality of darkness that exists in my soul. There is a notable absence of him when I am experiencing success, yet I repeatedly welcomed him into my best days. The real danger comes in not knowing whom you're dealing with. The difference in the states of mind that occupy you throughout life can be any range of peak to valley. He, "the other guy", is a pathological liar. He means well, as his intent is to balance our worlds, but he is unfit for compassion and logic. He sees the world as his infinite oyster and people as his infinite resource. He has no intentions on paying anyone back.

The most dangerous person is someone who doesn't know themselves, or, more importantly, what they're capable of. There is no doubt through the halls of Alcoholics Anonymous I have been able to identify my true character. I understand that I come across arrogant, high-and-mighty, preachy, rude, impatient, and perpetually on my platinum soapbox. I bring that knowledge with me to every conversation or situation I enter, and I will do so until the day I die. My gripe isn't with my true self, it's with the version of me that is self-seeking, or provoked through addictive behaviors… I call him, "the other guy" because I'm not quite sure who he is, and what he's doing inside me. He makes decisions that I would never make, and I find myself in places I would never bring myself to. This alter ego laughs at my compassion and human decency. He strips me of my humaneness. He will tell you anything you want to hear, but remember, the road to hell was paved with good intentions. His methods are useless, I've finally come to grips with. I've learned him well enough to know when he's steering the ship, and practiced escaping his control enough times to know I'd rather part ways, at this point. He's embarrassed me, and I accept my humility, today. Too many minutes and days have been thrown away, unnecessarily, to his warped version of reality. He's not getting any more minutes!

1440. Up until recently I never had a use for this number. Being

a superstitious cunt, you might think this would've passed my

ear at some point in 42 years, but it's a new one to me. 1440

represents the number of minutes there are in one day. This

represents a lot more to a recovered addict. 1440 represents a

number of revolutions I sat and counted seconds and ticks,

grinding my teeth, then wiping the sweat off my palms. 1440

snapshots of a madman. 1440 tests of human character versus a

physical necessity. 1440 opportunities to make the next 1440 an

easier one, with no promises. Promises are for religious folks.

Anything with a modicum of fanfare attached to it would be

nauseating for most, but I'm out of options. Getting 1440

minutes behind me, just once, was everything. Every trip to

start a new count is more defeating and bleak than the last,

more difficult to persevere. Every shortcut is more catastrophic than the last. Every failed attempt is a strike to our already bruised egos.

An addict will give you the 24-hour spiel and the one day at a time bullshit, but I always found that to be extremely torturous. A guy like me needs to go one minute at a time. One second at a time, even. I wish I could say I was an orphan, or came from a displaced home, or even an abusive one… But, I cannot. I was raised by two human beings that sacrificed every minute of every day for the success of their children. I am the product of blind ignorance. My own, without effort towards progress...I just intoxicate myself and carry on. See, inside my own mind I know there's a fucking lunatic running around, and any justification I can latch on to would be greatly appreciated. How many times does one need to catch themselves during the day saying to some other unwanted and strangely perverse version of themselves to *cool it* and even question the origin of some mental intrusions? My thoughts are horrible. I would estimate between thirty-to-fifty times per day. That's about how many times a completely fantastical, outlandish, or completely disgusting and disgraceful vision comes prancing through my mind each day. The difference between my sober and addicted self is that I can see, in my sobriety, the simple fact that they are outlandish. Copious amounts of drugs, mostly methamphetamines, is the catalyst for my warped reality.

When I was around fifteen-years-old, and tried marijuana for the first time with my buddy Nick Delucca after missing the school bus on purpose, I knew right then and there that a life of drugs was my destiny. I vowed to myself that I would use any narcotic incessantly and slobbishly until I was in my early 40s, where I could then stop and heal enough to live a healthy, long life and write a book exclaiming my wild adventures around the globe. Then, just sit back and make millions from there. None of that is actually true, but it would make a lot of sense.

Anyway, that's about the gist of it, however, now that I'm at the book writing part it's all coming back to me. Oh, I haven't seen that millions yet, either, but I am happy and life is slowing down to a point I can understand, or make sense of, at least.

I spent the ages of 30's to 40's high on methamphetamines while working and traveling. I was high throughout my twenties as well, just not on meth. Back then it was anything. Meth became my life, and first and second true loves all in one. It was my God, and my master. Methamphetamines, unfortunately, happens to be the most addictive and destructive substance on the planet. It raises the baseline of dopamine in the human brain fifteen times the normal limit while subjecting its user to life-numbing indifference and physical obliteration. That's not extra. It's the most accurate succession of words that exists to describe it. It turned me into a human zombie. There is still some reminders and scattered remnants even today, after almost a year clean, that I have yet a long way to go, in spite of a somewhat lucid mind, of my failing nervous system. My hands can't squeeze tightly or grab smooth objects any longer with surety. I get random neuron-displacement, I lose my sense of direction spontaneously and randomly. I haven't held a job for over a few months in years due to a chronic misperception of myself professionally, and I haven't paid a penny of rent through that time, or ever, for that matter. I never paid my rent. It's how I fed my habits. I was a walking dead man and I thought I had everyone fooled. I heard and saw the sideways glances and caution in people while dealing with the sick version of me, a meth addicted lowlife. It hurt…it's part of what keeps me sober. I can promise in my lucid mind and feel it so vehemently in my heart, what a just and decent man I am, but my actions, high on drugs or not, are what I'm accountable for. I'm accountable as a father and carry the shame of my past at times. It grounds me when I get the itch or visions or delusions of grandeur. I would use the warmest hearted people and consume every last resource they had, because I gained their trust, before I left them for dead, stranded in random places without an outlet. Dead battery, no charger, or just a smashed, broken phone…coaxed on a promise of money or love and left with nothing. I, or should I say, "the other guy," left people with as little as he could. I was a heartless predator. I was never a violent or sexually deprived person, so I never was a prime candidate for a serial case but take away the aesthetics and I am nothing more than a death row convict that was fortunate enough to not need to take what I needed. I always got it. That's my outlier and the scariest part about me.

The scariest part is that I'm a dad. I fear my penance will be too great, kidnappings withstanding. I factor in the emotional grief of having endured losing a place in my daughter's life twice, and

I still have an immeasurable debt to my past. I am prepared...I think.

Originally, I experienced meth while living abroad in Southeast Asia, so the geographical cure in returning to the US saw me gain some traction in life and success for almost five years. I thought I had escaped. I could almost taste the drug regularly during those five years simply by writing its name or drumming up a fantasy laced memory. I had left my exotic life, living, working, and traveling through some of Asia's most beautiful islands. I had established structure and found a partner I could have lived with forever.

What happened over those five years was not a full surrender to the substance that brought me to my lowest form of humanity....to a cancer-like existence. I was the anti-solution. My mind dismissed the chance to ever get the drug, thus, rendering me to conformity of the best version of the life I was living - WITH THE CONTINGENCY THAT I WAS NOT LEAVING METH, I WAS LEAVING DEFEAT THROUGH OPPORTUNITY. I should have surrendered and trained my mind how toxic it is when I had the chance. Meth was always welcomed back into my life after I escaped its readily available status. I just never knew it. Once methamphetamines found their way to New England I was a dead man. I made it, thus far, but that has been by nothing more than chance. That was a scenario I never had the notion to anticipate or expect. My addicted self helped me dispel that notion without my authentic self realizing. Life was progressing along so perfectly. Fool me once, shame on you, fool me twice, shame on me. I went back down the road I knew was the most arduous and torturous....again. That last relapse lasted three years. I am now almost a year and two novels into my new, impenetrable life. "The other guy" inside me has had a 25 year sample size of opportunity to keep authentic me working and behaving properly while he gets his fix, meth. I've come to finally realize that it's just not going to be possible, so I permanently broke up with him. I said goodbye. I knew it was over from the start, but he kept telling me how he changed, how he was getting things together and how we could live in complete utopian bliss together, forever. I was always that guy that stayed in relationships with girls I couldn't stand for way longer than I should have, because I hate hurting people's feelings, and for my sexual conveniences. I would fulfill my needs elsewhere once necessary, as most dickheads would. I stayed because it was more comfortable than upsetting the balance of life. Even though the balances always tip, I never knew when it would, just when I wasn't ready to hear it.

My addicted self, "the other guy," put me in every awful situation I ever experienced. He doesn't know boundaries. He knows pain, craziness, torture, and warp speed. The way people would look at me with pity while I was outside, ragged and rundown from the night before... I can remember all of them. I never cared how they felt about me, I cared how I felt about me. I hated me. I hated "the other guy" that goes into a gas station for a crack pipe at 6am while the rest of the universe is off getting it done, all so I could fix the shakes I had, or the overwhelming anxiety and self-loathing from coming down. I would lower my eyes and shake my head...at myself. It was like looking at myself, living one questionable moment after another, through my own eyes from the bottom of my stomach weighted down by my awful decisions while a madman had the wheel. That's not to say I would be claiming insanity had I ever been tried and convicted of a crime, but there's no question that my authentic character, integrity, and self-respect I believe I embody, looks at the actions of my addicted self with pity and shame... and, fear. Fear is what healed me. Fear is something I hadn't felt since I started taking drugs, and that's how I knew. I guess any fear for me would be considered healthy and welcome. I remember sitting on the back porch of a three-family home I was leasing the ground floor of, chatting with a pimp, the uncle of the 17-year-old girl I was about to hire for an hour of sex-filled fantasies, and thinking it would be a good idea to offer them the spare room in the house in exchange for daily pleasure. The pimp was carrying a crack pipe and a pistol and had another young girl waiting in the car, and all this seemed okay. That was a normal day in my addicted life. That is the absence of fear, and quite frankly looking back, pure fear in itself!

The guy I saw looking back at me while I was off doing horrible things was a disgrace of a human being. He took the easy way out of every situation. I know he never looked anyone in the eye, because he left me with the guilt of it. He left me with a lot of guilt. The beauty in the journey comes from within. It's my soul's perpetual healing and the small signs along the way that tell me, I'm doing this the right way now. It's a universal reward earned through right actions. I'm not one of those Alcoholics Anonymous blowhards that tells myself to put down the bat or to love myself, or even to forgive myself. I am well aware of the 12 steps of recovery (not that I refute it), but I rescinded my own membership. Apparently, one fuck up there and you start all over. I've been around the block enough times to know that if I keep going around the block it's always going to be the same distance of a ride. I have a massive disconnect with the perfectionists' perspective of recovery. I'm just looking to stay away from drugs, not to be a Saint on Earth. I enjoy my mistakes as long as they don't negatively affect another human. I understand that I used drugs like a pig. I understand that once "the other guy" has his switch turned on, then all else is purely up to chance. At least, in the early going. I don't need to be surrounded by those in recovery to remember how sick I am. I need to free myself with the knowledge of who I am in any given moment. That is where I cure my disease.

I spent the first 30 years of my life expecting to handle things on my own, refusing help from every offer, and thus, suffering. It's okay to ask for help, I understand. Now I do, at least. I would assume anybody could understand the frustrations in dealing with the society of people who believe their word should just be accepted and the mark of their character is measured by their intentions. There is this wide presumption in America that we are better than the next person, and that our needs are primal. To us, they are… and that is justification enough for most Americans. As a culture, we avoid conflict but promote war and violence. We encourage logic, yet encourage every American to act on their feelings, and that those feelings are valid. Feelings alone are not valid. The only thing that can be valid is the reason you feel that feeling, but a feeling should never be another person's problem. Feelings are for us alone to navigate through and grow from. It's our connection to other humans, not our differences, that promotes a positive outcome to our feelings, misplaced or not. It's our own responsibilities to get that first 1440 behind us, no matter what it takes. It took throwing my meth dealer and two prostitutes out of my house on September 28, 2021 after my daughter was abducted for the second time, and my meth dealer was filling her crayon boxes with methamphetamines. That's who "the other guys" is, and that is why he's no longer welcome.

Who am I? That is a question that cannot be answered with the next thought in my mind. It can't be answered with the next words that pass through my lips or the next intention that flows through my body. I am a slob. Most of my friends like to use the phrase "adulting," but I wouldn't even know what that is or where to start. I like to break it down simpler for my singed brain… I call it "lifing." If you ask anyone who they are, they will most likely give you a dissertation on what they do for a living, and what the status is at their home or bank, and how many children they have, or brothers and sisters they have, or even something they may have accomplished most recently. That's not who I am. I am a product of my actions. Who am I? I am an irrelevant human, forced to stay small for my own protection. I am a self-seeking predator and a complete life slob. I am the result of all the resources I've sheepishly and selfishly consumed, all the hearts that I've mangled, and all the souls that I've crushed. I am a guiltless father who is watching his child suffer at the hands of his addiction, unapologetically. I am a bully and a scam artist. These are my actions. This is who I am. I'm not these things without intent otherwise, but at the end of the day… this will be on my résumé. I am an emotionless sociopath when it comes to death. I am incapable of hurting anything knowingly, but I have, and I will again, because I'm human.

We live in a world growing increasingly larger in population, yet growing increasingly less experienced in human emotion and interaction. We've taught ourselves that it's okay to be afraid of the person standing next to you, that there's potential danger in any situation. We've taught ourselves how to defend ourselves against another human, but not how to love one. The digital versions of ourselves we've created over the past decade have done human beings a major disservice. People firmly believe they are who they purport to be digitally, thus, forfeiting any opportunity for that person to have the ability to self-assess, and more importantly, to self-accept life as it exists outside of a glowing monitor. **That** is the saddest thing to me.

My belief is that the reason people do this is because in social circles it's unclear to us until much later in life how we come across to others. Behavioral science attributes it to self-esteem issues or a range of male dominant afflictions, but it's really just curiosity and boredom, in most cases. We, as humans, have a hard time relating to emotion we can't physically see. We can't even "see" ourselves properly, or as our peers do. I thought I was so much more subtle and less obnoxious than I really am. It took me almost four decades to get it through my head.

We have our own vision of what we'd like to be perceived as, but we can't really be sure, with the sample size so small, of the accuracy in our youth. We need validation. We find whatever validation we need online while our social circles are growing smaller as time goes on. I can remember back when I was a child having at least eight to ten friends I would gallivant the neighborhoods endlessly with, while keeping an ear out for my father yelling, calling me home (his yell was believed to stretch all the way to the river). My friends would often come peddling frantically around the connected neighborhoods through river trails and beyond even their own parentally monitored boundaries to see if I was there, trying to warn me that he was calling, helping me to dodge a beating. They didn't care if they had plans or were doing something. People, generally speaking, would give you any time you wanted when I was young. I can't get an *excuse me* out before my addressee has hurriedly hastened his or her pace, and tunnel visioned their ass right past me, looking back in worry. I never thought I'd see the day when people thought someone engaging in amicable dialogue would be worrisome.

Back in the old neighborhood, I ventured beyond my dad's sound waves with regularity, just to see what color ass whipping I would be getting, or the even more adrenaline packed resolution, making it back within earshot before he or my mom knew I breached the perimeter of his voice, and thus, dodged the spanking. We still would go looking for random mischief, close to home or not. The fear of punishment didn't stop me even as a child. Another 8 to 10 friends I kept close with at my elementary school would share weekends (the ones I wasn't grounded for) with me. We alternated sleepover destinations and played floor hockey and tried our damn best to make it through Saturday Night Live, back when Steve Martin and Chevy Chase were regulars and Adam Sandler was just a pimply New England Jew. I don't even see eight to ten kids playing in any neighborhood these days. I haven't seen a pickup street hockey game or whiffleball game in a decade. I haven't had an unexpected knock on my door or ring on my doorbell for years. People might just grab their firearm before answering an unexpected visit to their home in 2022. We have changed so much, so quickly.

We, as humans, are the last ones to notice change in ourselves, physically or mentally. Basically, if ten people tell you you're an asshole, you're an asshole! Just blindly accepting it rather than finding ways to let it offend you will release you from self-bondage. We have a mental perception of ourselves that we would like to maintain within our social groups, but the execution of that character often falls short, and even further from reality in our youth. We fill our digital profiles, myself included, with random humans whose thumbnail photos have piqued our interest enough to click a button. This creates some sick sense of fulfillment, admittedly in me too. Who hasn't said to themselves *I'm just clicking a button?*" Insert shrug emoji. If the opposite of addiction is connection, then getting out of our comfort zones and being the change we would like to see is paramount for our development and evolution as a species.

Hiding behind a digital persona will just exacerbate our current state of affairs; a state of humanity in deep need of connection. The reality of our timeline in humanity and its subsequent continued success is entirely contingent on the action of our greater masses, not our leaders. Staying authentic and firmly planting our feet into our own realities is now a practiced asset. Our beloved Internet and World Wide Web are now the forums for our character, thus, deeming irrelevant, or seemingly so, our day-to-day actions. There's no doubt that technological advances can be beneficial to all of our species, but the way we employ our false personas into our digital profiles seems to be holding a lot of us back. There's no more believable lie than the ones we tell ourselves.

The fact is, we all want nothing more than to convince ourselves of how well we're doing. We, myself included, do it to create a momentary boost in my own self-esteem, so I can avoid a life bereft of perpetual stimulation. I struggled a long time with knowing my imperfections and the unattractive parts of my character, but never fully being able to accept it. There's a difference in being able to recite what my flaws are and accepting that they may have had a negative impact on a situation, and then becoming accountable, remorseful, and assertive in a positive solution. I would let my ego strip me of my vulnerability by not allowing myself to be wrong and happy. All for what? To say I was right and maintained my faux pride? It sounds asinine when I put it on paper, but it's natural instinct in more people than it's not. There is no victory in unnecessary contention. Unimaginable bonds are built when I break my walls down and let other people in.

I've convinced myself, while high on meth and many other substances, that my life was second to none. A premium example of first-class human existence. I was a toxic, dangerous, broke ass piece of shit, but my mind told me I was crushing it. This isn't exclusively symptomatic in addicts so much as it is humans. It may just be a bit more magnified in us addicts. Either way, the focus is the problem. We beat ourselves to an emotional pulp when we feel awful and attack like a starved, rabid spider monkey when we see light. It's our, addicts, responsibility to recognize where we need to improve without making it an internal revolution, but internal evolution. The oft failed balancing act lies between recognizing our areas of realignment in our character and energy, and taking the slow and healthy action needed to overcome.

I use the word douchebag, cunt, fuck, pussy, rctard, dipshit, fucktard, loser, weirdo, donkey dick, and faggot. I have no problem with any word used in proper context. I don't use these words to hurt anyone, because it's up to you how you let the irrelevance of sound make you upset. I use racial slurs, too.

Make no mistake about it. Every race has their outcasts, these derelicts emulating the indignant path of their race's ignorants. I just know you're rejoicing in "I fucking hate this guy" at my over-the-top ignorance, but I couldn't care less. I don't see things as ignorant because of the impact of my sounds to other's feelings. My actions aren't negotiable or amenable contingent upon what is said to me. Words help. They help every situation, if you listen. The level of impact of a particular word's "harshness", or the stress of a syllable, or a bilabial lingual ingressive click, or kissing sound, will never force you to feel anything. The feelings we get are from the adrenaline and shock and emotional entitlement our bodies and minds experience when we hear these things. So, in complete actuality, it's impossible to be hurt by sounds. We hurt ourselves. I'll never be a member of the "words hurt" committee. All words hurt. Impactful words only hurt as much as you let them hurt. I choose to understand someone feeling the need to let out their anger, or ignorance, for that matter. If all the doctors encourage us to express our emotions; how can it be only the emotions socially accepted? We would have to be accepting of the entire range of emotions, justified or not, to be congruent.

I'm not looking to go through life perfectly, obviously. I am looking to go through life happily. I'm pretty sure any day of my life can be marked up with a red pen in several different areas. That just means I'm human. If my version of happy means crossing the verbal boundaries that some of you hold in such high regard, then so be it. My legacy isn't going to be built on the words that I used, it'll be built on the actions I've made. There's a large percentage of people who feel otherwise, or pretend to so they can cling to their "get out of life-jail free" card. We're constantly being told that our feelings are valid, but now we're validating them in the workplace, and schools, and home. Our feelings are what get us in trouble and leave us disappointed. Our feelings are the impact of expectations, those met and those ignored. Feelings now trump procedure, protocol, policies, schedules, obligations, and even laws at times. Americans carelessly throw their feelings and their children's lives to shield their horrifically out of character decisions. I'm not sure when the general consensus tipped the scales in the American governmental party that lost its nutsack, but I'd like to see 'tough love' start trending back up. I guess that makes me a Republican? Who knows, but I did vote for Trump.

The English language is one of the most complex and creative languages in the universe. There is a multitudinous alternative to any word in our language, yet we cling to the ones that impact our feelings to take umbrage with, and damn the speaker. "Cunt" is a tough one but having lived with and befriended several Aussies and Kiwis (New Zealanders), I have made *cunt* my *fuck,* and made *fuck* my *hello, thank you, excuse me, I'm sorry, and*

I love you. Whatever, I'm over it. I notice every set of eyes in the room when I say that word, and I know immediately who my people are, and who to avoid. Now, while I understand this doesn't necessarily put me in the best position to gain friends, I don't believe my verbiage should be a prerequisite to assessing my character. It's a reflection of my feeling and opinion. My actions are a reflection of my character. I guess, to make my point, I'm just not interested in being friends with anyone that thinks lesser of me because of my words. American's natural inclinations towards instant gratification, even in acquiring friends, is repulsive enough to see through the spineless and ween out the herd. I enjoy having a circle between ten and twenty people, family included, that I give everything to, as needed; physically, emotionally, and financially. They, in return, because I genuinely value their existence, pay me back tenfold.

Here's where I become a hypocrite: I'm writing about my opinions, through addiction, in hopes of helping somebody whose mind does what mine does. I may be crazy, but I am far from alone. I understand completely that by writing something that gets mass published and holds nothing back, I am, essentially, contradicting my life's intention and what I'm imploring more of you **not** to do. Sometimes it's a matter of prioritizing my intention, and the potential benefit of helping another human far outweighs the potential for anyone to think that I'm a hypocrite. I get the irony. The irony in this entire thought; if you, reading this, now start to feel as though I may be hypocritical, you are right. However, the word "hypocrite" is defined as pious, or purporting to be more noble, or better than. Integrity is the counter to Hypocrisy. My intention is clearly one of integrity, yet I am seemingly holding myself in higher nobility by trying to help because I am in a better position than some of the more seriously active and afflicted? I get it's a stretch, but the benefit of many far outweighs the shame of one.

With the endless answers to the world tucked in each of our pockets, it becomes increasingly harder to be a bad person and get away with it. It's harder with modern forensics to commit crimes, harder for boyfriends to cheat on girlfriends, and harder to create a false alibi. What I never realized is how narrow people are getting. I understand the conformity, yet inside me nothing finds any appeal in conformity. I may not quite be someone thought of as a bad person, but I'm at least known for doing highly questionable things. Bad things, to some. Exciting for me. I don't necessarily think I'll ever be one to use soft words or consider someone's feelings the way others do. To be honest, all we're becoming as a species is boring. Everything's been done… Everything's been created, analyzed, explored, named, dug up, flown through and to, and consumed. And with so much less left to discover, it's hard to picture where we will

be as time progresses into the next century in comparison to

centuries past when it comes to art, literature, and philosophy,

but it's inevitably racing towards us faster than we care to react.

I can't see the world being a good place to exist in decades to

come. I am a Darwinist, in addition, so I am equally optimistic

and intrigued about the potential of our existence as a species, I

just fear the priorities we manifest. I think I'd get a pretty good

show of hands if I was to ask who feels as though they were

born decades or centuries too late. I prefer simplicity. The

majority enjoys simplicity.....so, this begs the question: just

because we *can* do something, are we obliged to, as a smaller

part of a species of life that relies on that particular asset we

possess to further its existence? I vote…NO!

Maybe I'm wrong. Maybe we all, myself definitely excluded,

enjoy the perpetual insanity of trying to keep up with life in

America. In a world without advancement, there would be no drugs made in laboratories, good and bad. There would be no competition for jobs or forceful government. We wouldn't be complicating our laws driven by media and big business. We wouldn't be fearing the worst-case scenario, because we wouldn't know what that was. We wouldn't have it broadcasted in every glowing device every minute of every day. We would appreciate hardship and physical endurance. We would go back to having broader hopes and more time spent with people, not tasks or devices. We would go back to being the best version of ourselves… a person we don't even know exists. We would go back to knowing each other.

Since that's never going to happen, because the *self* outweighs the greater picture, almost always, we'll have to keep making the best of what we're given. I forcefully implore acceptance into my head. It's the best way and only way I can free myself from myself. I remind myself…. again, I'm powerless over any noun. My happiness isn't attached anymore to what I'm looking to receive in life as much as it's attached to the quality of the moments I encapsulate and inspire in, teach and be taught in, and see and listen through, wholeheartedly. Age brings us to a place, like it or not, where the moments go slower and time moves faster. We start to intuitively understand our legacy and where we will have the greatest opportunity for positive impact. Wisdom is a generic word categorized by age, and to some degree, it's true. We make better decisions after years of failed risks. We know the level of risk that matches our level of acceptable consequences. We know better the way the systems of existence work; car registrations, mortgage loans, unemployment claims, and all the nuances and idiosyncratic tasks to getting through a normal American day along the way. We are less frustrated because we have experienced frustration….and it didn't help. We are simple, yet perpetually adapting. We are stronger and more capacitated as a species as time goes on. We are more motivated, but less willing. We have found a means to tie up those daily obligations and legally sign from the palm of our hands, thus, freeing up our time to be more than we ever have been able to in generations past. We are evolving still and even faster as people become less restricted. Babe Ruth, for instance, standing at only a modest 6'1", would most likely get cut from his high school's varsity team in 2022. Maybe it's a stretch to project mediocrity, but his size and stature alone wouldn't warrant a second glance. Everything evolves physically and academically. Emotionally we are devolving because there is no tangible measure to emotional growth. We have let go of our compassion towards others, and we have been given the justifications by our past professors and scholars. Emotional boundaries are only for a few exceptions in our lives. Constantly growing is that pool of humans we encounter through the phases of life we pass through.

Perpetually shrinking are our boundaries without warning or possessing the mindfulness to know that we're doing it.

I often wonder how I even let myself get this deep in concern that I let it affect my day or my time. Writing, as I mentioned, is entirely hypocritical in some eyes, but it's my beacon of hope to other addicts, helpless dads, and people that just want to be reminded of what an aspiringly flawed human sounds like. I'd be happy dying with a hand in all those flawed jars. Addicts are socially the most polarized of that group, but paradoxically hard to imagine when one category literally says aspiringly flawed humans, but acknowledgement and acceptance sound alike to most, but are far from synonymous. Addicts are still going to need way more help than the rest, but that help can come from one place only, and the end of that road is as elusive as enlightenment. It comes from a place in our soul that seeks redemption harder and faster and longer than "the other guy" in us can run. A place that doesn't just recite our part in our own demise, but a place that resonates acceptance in our own redemption. Redemption eludes even the best of us because we never make it to a point where "the other guy" lets us remember and feel the person we are away from his clutches.

I am a father, a son, a brother, a resource, a friend, a boyfriend, a stepparent, a farmer, a writer, a chef, and a human being. These are the titles that you can apply to my name and my legacy. They will never be a testament to my character, and that is why I get myself to the next day. My character is what makes me all those things. I will never be free from the fact that my character is that of two people; me and "the other guy." The only way we shed any of those titles is through our true selves. The real *me* needs to stay ahead of him, projecting his whereabouts and forecasting his insidious infection of my vulnerability.

4 | Date My Digital Self

Incubus/Succubus

Nouns: a male/female demon believed to have sexual intercourse with women/men while they sleep.

Throughout my social engagements I almost feel responsible to affect your life in such an impactful way where you can draw two parallels to your existence in the sand. One before you knew me and one after. Throughout my intimate relationships I have been the stark opposite. Give me an out or opportunity to show you a new level of self-sabotage and I'll take it. It's not to say there isn't or wasn't an impactful moment during the self-sabotaging process, but that wasn't my aim. That stuff happens when people place an inaccurate mark on their own importance in the world or to another. I can't explain this phenomenon; maybe it's the temporary status my social acquaintances carry with them that help me grasp the ease in acquiring friends or the smothering permanence of a significant other free that makes the latter far less manageable. Either way, I haven't the slightest clue as to who that person is within the self-sabotaging headspace that becomes my persona when I feel the itch to get out a relationship, but he, too, is obviously a part of me and a part that perpetually teeters between the lucid and inebriated mindsets that I can't ever remove myself from employing to do my bidding. He has given me the scientific soundness in my addiction as a disease as it infiltrates areas removed from substance. He teaches me about me....as does every intimate situation I enter.

A pernicious predation of our culture is upon us…and has been. It lies in the noctivagant form of online dating. This I have experienced with my own two eyes, my slim wallet, and my obnoxious stance that people are genuinely genuine. I've dabbled myself in the self-seeking portals of *Match.com, Plenty of Fish, Tinder, etc.* What I didn't realize was how contrived and misled the sites and situations stemming from these sites were. Men and women claiming cultural evolvement have polluted their homes and their lives through these portals on a magnificent level. All for the sake of not dying alone do men and women risk their current lifestyles to engage with strangers that have created an online profile to gauge the level of compatibility between each other, and therefrom subject themselves to repeated and tireless self-validation. I must have forgotten what fun sounded like for a spell.

My mid-thirties came littered with a gold or premium subscription to almost every dating app on the planet. I'm now in my early forties and officially removed from ever having to repurpose my efforts, and with my growing nostalgia comes the realization that many of the women I dated through those apps are still currently members. This means one of two things. One, they are catfishes; they are phishing for personal info to scam or they are made by employees of the site in order to draw traffic. Two, they are serial daters and have been misled by the existence of the internet. They have bitten hard on the "red flag" theory. They are the ones that go right to the customizable check sheet on the back page to mark up their unapologetic life boundaries before they cleverly guide you through the shrewd, no nonsense, seemingly to-good-to-be-true attitude, and energy their bios can purport, just in case anyone ever did read one before getting a private response. Most polled Americans would agree that a *bio* is a digital profile, at this point and not a summation of one's actual life. I have a hard time driving out to dinner with a list of everything I can't be while sitting down to a time lapsed, egregiously less appealing version of a digitally confident, extremely photogenic slob with a taste for Louis Vuitton. At the end of the day, men and women alike, appreciate a partner who doesn't mind being simply a hole on most days. A hole to fill our problems with a hole to fill our partner's privates with. Having a partner who understands human nature and respects the ebbs and flows of another's day is the greatest blessing in the world.

Most, almost 70% of members, have photos that can be stamped by years, like rings on a tree, digitally. I'm not sure how it's not the digital elephant in the digital chat room, or maybe it is. I always chose to move towards an agreeable solution than figure out where it went wrong. There is no benefit that can come simply by reiterating the problem or affixing blame. The solution is...none to speak of. These are people that I will never see eye to eye with. There is obviously no getting back the hope I once had in this person as a lover, but I never let that dismiss someone's importance to me as a friend, frenemy, cohort, colleague, or fuck friend. I never cared to categorize my people, just my person. My person is all of those. The undeniable fact and reasons behind why we are manufacturing our own internal bullshit to misrepresent ourselves to our intended life partner should be the first "ice breaking" couple's quiz and the start of online dater's self-assessment tools. The infuriatingly deceitful onset of a contrived meeting to become someone's life partner marks the first example of "sugar-coating" in a presumably transparent engagement. For most, it should mark the last, but human nature is to compare and match integrity, as we would anyone in an intimate setting, thus setting the stage from the start for an inevitable split.

Self-assessment is arguably the most essential tool to becoming our best self, yet the rarest character asset in even our most intellectual circles. Accurate and unfiltered self-assessment of my own character, good and bad, was the catalyst in me applying myself properly in the world. One major hurdle in trying my luck in the online dating pool was not only a general inability for my dates to self-assess, but their general lack of intuition and mental capacity. I guess you can say I fall in the sapiosexual category. That's actually a dealbreaker, so sapiosexuality is essentially the starting point, for me. Along with appearances, availability, grooming, smile, confidence, and libido. Libido; It's no laughing matter, but I've dated women that aren't even hookers where I still needed to plan, pay for, and 'earn' my sex. Everyone reserves the right to figure things out, but there is no resolve for those that place their feelings and status above all else and let their mood dictate their immediate surroundings. I haven't the patience for humans that reserve their feelings and distort their character for the purpose of not appearing too eager, or going against the societal grains. I need vulnerability and honesty, not protocol. I'm not sure Saint Peter has a checklist for socially acceptable courting practices at the entry gate to heaven, anyway.

Availability is something I grew to appreciate through my years living and working throughout Southeast Asia. I remember thinking how difficult it was for my best friend, Gino, to get a couple free hours on a weekend to get our kids together for playtime. I am always freed for my people, or I will find a way to be free for them at the earliest time. Life is busy, no doubt, but it's as busy as we fill it up to be. The level of importance people put on their arbitrary tasks in the United States is astounding. I needed a girl that could be ready and get mobile in a minute. Idle time is the devil's playground for an addict. Having a partner that compliments my lifestyle accounts for a massive part of my sobriety. I'm experienced enough in my repeated witherings to know that chasing a girl that I know is a definite bad idea will come back to bite me hard. It took up until recently for the pain of the consequences to finally outweigh the thrill of the chase and the validation my victory provided to myself and other men.

Physically coveting women is never going away and is the oldest and most carnal human instinct. Valuing her…my person's security in all areas while respecting her decisions is where I have lost so many. I am the type that has always allowed my partner to choose me. Always more fearful of rejection than hopeful to see where my efforts brought me, in my youth. I get incredibly sick of people and the time that takes grows shorter as I get older. I have found my partner and I did not meet her on a dating platform. We were actually high school friends, but my level of deplorability hardly made me tolerable to her until recently. Our dads were long time friends and Tammy, my partner for life, was married for twenty years to mister wrong while I gallivanted around the world in bachelor overdrive. Tammy heard every detail of my destructive path around the world - passed from our dad's third shift nights at Malden Mills together, to her. The comfort in not having to build up the patience to listen to another serial dater with a checklist scoffing at my over opinionated, self-deprecating story while questioning every decision I ever made….has no price tag. The transparency offered becomes a source of suspicion. I'm grateful for what I have, and it is only through time already lapsed and battles long since lost that I question my own competency in my former interest in meeting women the way I was. I was an incubus; never was the aim what I purported it to be, but the outcome always the same, and I wouldn't dare waste my time without the understanding that my physical needs, my addiction, would be immediately met. I can speak only for myself because I am emphatically sure I can acknowledge the addictive nature and inner turmoil my addicted self creates, but when something I do makes me truly feel worse, sad, guilty, or shamed; it always makes me feel the same way; addicted and alone. This is what addiction is. Knowing in my own mind that I don't have the ability, physically, to make the best decision for myself. When I surrender to the inevitable fight, preemptively at times, my alter ego puts up in it's shoe-stomping battle it's waging war against my personal integrity. The comprehensive set of values and level of compassion I was born with, not the one my addicted self wants. I admit guilt in premature dismissal when it comes to my feelings over another's, but I don't care. The alacrity in my expressions has eroded to unrecognizable levels. See, my second drug of choice is sex. Methamphetamine may have paved the road of true, healthy fear through life decimating, self-inflicted torture, but for a long time it encompassed everything I envisioned in my one true love; sexual fantasies, mind numbing, euphoric bliss, healthy focus, and guiltless anything (and I mean ANYTHING). If only I could have avoided the torture. One clever adage that stuck with me through my many attempts at sobriety has been "pain is inevitable, suffering is optional." The balance needs to be pinned to a healthy level in order to maintain the current path. The path of least resistance the road most often taken.

Refusing to accept my inabilities and sure-to-be failures was a bitter pill and one I still fight, at times. I believe every human has the ability to add something to the world without it owing them in return. That, I believe, is our basic obligation to each other. Be a giver. In a world that bears little forgiveness, a slow regression should still be considered a failed existence... perpetual progress should be every humans aim. While it's never going to be judged whether we choose mankind or our most immediate blood lines to focus our assets and attention on, as it's our unquestionable decision, and a decision that should have no expectations tied to it, it will be one we ultimately have to make. There is no longer the time in our contemporary societies to balance both with the reciprocity we aspire towards.

My partner is someone I want involved in, or welcome to be, any aspect of my life. Being the best version of me for my family through their vision, versus my own vision of what I believe I have to offer others, will never meet in the middle. I have accepted that. My family knows I love them and would eat a bullet for any one of them, but I believe they are better off seeing me help myself, and subsequently, other addicts.

Humans in general don't really understand the magnitude of anything that they have, be it a feeling or an object. It's easy to know what we don't want to lose, though. Life, loosely speaking, is a phasic journey. We set our boundaries based on what we know. The peaks and valleys are all relative to our circumstance on Earth. The reality is that we actually have zero idea what our limits, low and high, are. Looking back to my doting days, I recognized a pattern that encompasses the problem. The problem for me would always be trying to give any interest of mine the time in our dialogue to assess our compatibility honestly, applying transparency in my actions and honesty in my self assessment and current situation as it pertains to my level of interest, and a growing presumption, or skepticism, that everyone I meet must have something wrong with them, because I had so many things wrong with me. The modus operandi for online dater's is a chronic situation. It's a list of people filtering ideas or boundaries that they've established as part of their character. Basically, if you have a box to put a red flag on, then it's not me that's the problem. For every character defect, subjective by nature, that we forcefully apply to our intimate lives, renders us destined for a complete failure; not because we're looking for exactly what we want, but we're vetting people for what we don't want. There are so many attributes that can far outweigh any red flag, even in the most dismissive instances. Every preloaded question has an agenda. It's not a dialogue, but an interview. This is the unnatural direction that we've taken our existence?

Having absolute carnal knowledge that I am and going to be a ragingly addicted human until the day I die, I can honestly attest that my involvement with these sites was purely predicated on short term stimulation for a hypo-maniac and sex addict. I am a predator without a physically harmful intention. I aim at your character and feelings. I consume the female resources because I covet the next high...sexual release. Much like my trips home from my dealer's house after getting my bag of drugs, succeeding in the ultra sensitive race to a woman's vagina before she exposes your true self is the high. It is the drug. Most addicts can identify with having pure contentment in their high before the drug has entered our bodies. It's real. Once the chase has a conclusion the human mind takes care of the celebration and anxiety immediately dissipates.

Having been a devout student of AA once upon a time, I can recite the suggestions and the absolute "nos" an alcoholic is allowed to mouth. Addicts, naturally, having a leery disposition and instinctual disdain towards authority in general, would have had several "uh-oh" moments up until this point in the read, but I don't give a fuck what you or other addicts think of me, I care what you know about me. I know myself more than a program does. I respect it and do my best and have stopped measuring myself against people, circumstances, and former versions of myself. I am unburdened by doing this. I know where and when I'm negotiating with my disease because I couldn't ever conform to the level the program suggests, and I know where and when I'm behaving "soberly", proudly. Having this practiced self-check-in ability is where I found my first semblance of true sobriety success.

Celibacy and abstinence are two foreign words to me, so the fact that I can now look behind me and accept that I was a predator on those dating sites, feeding my disease while it convinced me I just needed a good girl in my life, searching for my next release of dopamine. Science and math don't lie. They help a guy like me make sense of the cart careening out of control.

5 | Capital Gains…Punishment

It may be hard to imagine me questioning more of the life passing by me, I know……as a species, our greatest leaders have set laws and governments are elected to lead us, the people, through the powerful majority voice of the people. The majority of normal people don't want or accept without juxtaposition its governing authority to overextend its perceived control.

One facet of our social structure is how ineffectively we pour money into the programs with the highest, most sensitive liabilities. We dump money into substance abuse recovery resources rather than preventative measures or aftercare. We offer little to no state funding for aftercare programs compared to what inpatient programs get. Rehab facilities claim epic success rates because there is no statute other than the next 24 hours to an addict. Everyone leaves rehab clean. They prey on the weak and vulnerable. Almost ALL addicts remain clean through inpatient rehabilitation, yet between 80-90% of those treated in inpatient centers have a relapse in the first year. It's our self-will run riot out in a world we're trying to run away from, left to our own repeatedly failed devices, that brings us addicts back to the chase. If anyone had an idea what our governments were footing the bill for... you would be shocked. Tens of billions of dollars annually. Our aftercare workers are struggling to make ends meet themselves while traveling to remote personal homes to care for and spend time with addicts in their height of craving and the restructured hollowness they're left to crawl up from. The $60,000 the rehab charged for some goat yoga and equine therapy and a fake diploma could have paid two aftercare employees for one year to connect us back to the life we know we want, but can't find the way there. The widely used *TED Talks* adage that goes *the opposite of addiction is connection*, egregiously contradicts the general notion of an inpatient rehabilitation facility. We remove the addict from one warped reality into another; a fluffy, structured environment with peers of our own kind, discussing our efforts in having landed there or having emotional support counselors and family filled weekends where the families get patted down like the addict.

Horse ranchers even stick their hands into the grossly disproportionate allocation of state funds and offer addicts a day a week to spend sitting on an old, rickety, retired Clydesdale...and addicts spending twenty-four-hours over thirty days while all jumping at the chance to take the rehab van to see the horses. I did so while I was there. I'm a one and done kinda guy, though. I find it better that way, but most insurances cover at least two-to-three inpatient stays for addicts. I did love it there. Although most clinicians at state funded rehabilitation facilities are licensed it isn't necessary to work the position with a certification. Many of the counselors are nothing more than recovering addicts and former students. It's like those *Hair Club for Men* commercials where the client is also the president. Rehabs are taking advantage of their own clients and using them to increase their profit margins. They're being paid more than 50% less than what a licensed clinician would make, thus, furthering the profit provided by taxpayer dollars. I, personally, have always found recovery groups more beneficial when spearheaded by a former addict or someone in recovery. It's hard to identify with normal people.

That being the case, fair wage is another failing problem in this country. The minimum requirement of $7.25 in New Hampshire is roughly $300 pre-taxed dollars a week on a full-time salary. That's $1200 pre-taxed dollars a month and not enough for even a room at a rooming house with the necessary amount of food. We've seen Covid cut millions of jobs from our workforce. Those jobs are still readily available, but we've allowed our own citizens the ability to live without working. Massachusetts, for instance, will provide up to $3000 for a prostitute that makes $3000 a week cash by marketing her "assets" over online portals. Personally, I got kicked off Facebook for telling someone I was going to punch them in a private message. Every memory I ever had of my daughter and all the photos we took, memories we shared….all now in digital cyberspace, but we can't block hoes from selling their vaginas online? I guess it's a far stretch for a complaint, but it's merely just a scope of our priorities as a nation. If the feelings are instantly and negatively impactful, then we're told to shut it down. It's obviously a matter of priority. We prioritize the appearance of being decent over actually being so. We're slowly becoming the new Amsterdam with our relaxed efforts with marijuana, without protest from me, but again, the government is adding over 12% to the taxes to build back the communist regime. The beauty of a communist government is they actually give the money back to the people. Not on the state-by-state basis, but as a country as a whole. Communism sounds much better than the current state we're living in…economic and ethical blindness.

I went to a mountainside drug and alcohol rehabilitation facility in central Massachusetts in the Fall of 2018. I had just informed my boss I had taken over $48,000 cash from him and spent it all on drugs and hookers. It was rehab or jail. I came out of rehab singing the tunes of sobriety and blabbering like a doofus about all the spirituality I discovered in myself and how much progress I made over 30 days. That's the obnoxious cunt I was telling you about. Anyway, long story short, I was pinched for a DUI and got fired from that same company some five months after rehab. I guess I wasn't as spiritual as I thought.

Outside the controlled environment of a structured rehab, our addiction waits patiently….it lurks in the seediest corners of our souls and pries us from our happy lives, for a run of terror. It surrenders itself to our newfound structure and knows when it's outmanned. It is smarter than our well -intended, normal mindsets. Just as much as addictive minds feel contentment before ingesting our drug of choice, it knows equally as well when we have no opportunity to ease it, and it makes sure not to poke a sleeping bear, our rapidly healing, sober self. It waits for that version of us to need it again, and it consoles us every time…without fail. It waits for us to wreak of vulnerability again. Until the pain it causes is outweighed by the contrary, once again. Repeat.

Some addicts call detox or rehab a spin dry or a system flush. They get arrested, then court ordered and are on the streets with a warrant out for their arrest before they can complete their program. The alcohol and drugs haven't beat them down enough; arrest warrants and more of the same sound like a good idea. Insanity at its finest. Courts order addicts into these facilities to help them gain, at the very least, a small sample size and semblance of normalcy. There is no playbook or textbook for handling an addict, but it's safe to say that we can't help one that doesn't want help. The firm truth is that we all want help, but our disease scares us into thinking we're not going to survive without it. It plants scenarios in our mind of intolerable torture through abstinence. It plays the monotony tape forward and tells us we're victims. It manipulates us, and me, hard.

Now, after knowing these truths, how can we as human beings and compassionate beings continue putting a broken record on the turntable and pushing the pin in it? No one balks at it because all of their personal and professional liabilities are covered. The actual well-being of the suffering human is irrelevant, as long as the state has covered all their obligatory bases. And I hate being the whistleblower, but there are over 2 million untreated addicts walking the streets of The United States right now. These are the predators that people fear. These are the people, in complete transparency, we should be afraid of. It's not to say that any of them are bad people, but I've seen what drugs make me do, and it's not pretty. Like I said earlier, there's no difference between the way my brain works and the brain of a serial killer. I just haven't been deprived of my drugs of choice in a way that pushes me over the edge. I've had all the same thoughts, but I haven't followed through. The actual bad people are the ones committing these heinous crimes without the aid of hallucinogenic or mind-altering substances. In most cases, if not all, these people deemed unfit for society have been deemed so due to the involvement of substance in their life. Most often, the parents are chronic drug abusers.

My experiences through work and life have stretched around the globe. Most of them have been in Third World civilizations throughout Southeast Asia. Through my travels I found myself overseeing six hotels and casinos in the Philippines. While stationed in Cebu as my central location and premier property, I traveled around the country often, getting to see just about all of the country and its beauty. The Philippines is comprised of over seven thousand beautiful islands. Traveling isn't easy or cheap in the Philippines, but it's not hard to see where a once beautiful country of hardworking, humble people existed. What's left of the Philippines is nothing more than ruins. There have been no tsunamis or monsoons to help create the ruins and lengthen the rebuild process. The influence of foreign power, most specifically the United States, Is the reason the Philippines is in the shape they're in. The current situation in the Philippines is sad, to say the least. Manila, the capital, is overrun with squatters and meth addicts in every corner and seedy alley. Every block has billboards with naked 18- to 20-year-old girls wallpapered to the front of the building. Most of these girls no longer work inside these rooms, as the business doesn't always celebrate long-term success. Most women in the Philippines go to work in go-go bars as prostitutes between the ages of seventeen and nineteen years old. By the time they're twenty years old they have a slanted view and reluctance towards certain situations from the predators they've had the pleasure to experience the company of over the first couple years working the streets and the bars. Women widely accept infidelity by their partner and drugs are openly accepted as part of life.

The most fascinating detail about the current state of the Philippines economy is that the hardship was directly caused by the United States. It wasn't something we didn't do, it was something we did. The United States relinquished their control in the early 1900s, fully vacating in the mid 1960s, and established a democracy that saw them elect an American backed candidate and dictator-like, cancer of a man into the seat of Presidency, Ferdinand Marcos. Marcos, ironically, was born on September 11th, the most memorable day on the calendar for most Americans. The poverty laced streets and concrete jungle boulevards are a wreckage from former president Ferdinand Marcos. Marcos not only stole every penny he could from his position of power, but his insurgents slaughtered anyone who opposed him, media was only allowed to broadcast his approved messages starring mostly him and his film star and singer wife, Imelda Marcos. He was said to have imprisoned or killed over 110,000 of his own countrymen in fear they may rally up enough opposition support to overthrow him. His campaign and seat at the head were sponsored by our own American government, but because there is no oil or lithium in the Philippines…only Dole bananas, then we turn our eye to the situation and let them take their own training wheels off.

Marcos, elected in 1965, then self-designated by implementation of martial law in a democratic government for the next twelve years, served until he was overthrown after stealing almost ten billion dollars from the hardworking people of the Philippines and ducked the money into US bank accounts. The people of the Philippines widely regard their former leader as an authoritarian and kleptocrat. A kleptocrat, for those of you that would like to avoid picking up your phone and googling it, is just a ruler who uses his power for personal and financial gain. Marcos was solely responsible for the complete annihilation of his own country's relevance and ability to survive. His chronic vanity and incessant greed were so blinding that he missed the purposeful potential of his existence. How does one not find the eternal reward in helping not one, but millions of people and people alike. What I found in my one-year contract, a meth induced nightmare, was how impoverished and destitute the country was. I hadn't responsibilities in all the major regions of the Philippines, so my contract allowed me extensive travel. Every province was worse than the next. Parents offering their thirteen and fourteen-year-old daughters for any predator's sexual pleasure. It would be offered out for any amount of money. Any amount. As much as five dollars in the Philippines is enough for a family to eat for a few days. The drug infested boulevards in Cebu and Manila were enough to keep me in my room most nights. Squatters with red eyes you would see concealing metal objects and cash exchange kiosks would shut down by nightfall. Drouths of young women flock to karaoke parlors, beer gardens, and any other common place of commiserating for foreigners hoping to make a few dollars, all the while alert and fearful. A life no one should ever have to live. This is the life Marcos, an American ally created for his own country. A nation that elected him as their leader, dressed and spun with all the hope and promise of his promise to make his nation an equal and sister government, and economy comparable to the standard of American living at that time. Hundreds of millions of human beings going heartbroken and empty from the betrayal of their revered leader.

The friends I made while living in Thailand cautioned me to stay away from the South and avoid Davao, and that my relationships would be stronger towards the North, as I was raised Catholic, and the country is predominantly Catholic, but predominantly Muslim in the South. Religion never had any bearing on my friendships, but I can understand why those that hold it in a higher priority slot would think that way. The southernmost regions are Muslim. My resort was in Davao, a large, dusty coastal city in Mindinao, Philippines. Muslim communities were more prevalent in Mindinao down to the southernmost islands in Zamboanga. The Filipinos warned me, but always insisted that I take it at my own merit. Having done that, I found the southernmost regions of the Philippines to be the most desirable and attractive. The people are clear and polite. There are no squatters on every boulevard as there are in every other region of the Phils. You find no foreign predators lurking, preying on the young women trying to get their families out of poverty by compromising their integrity and shaming them in front of their families. People are just kind and unexpectedly outgoing and gregarious. I found a strong bond with my kitchen staff in that hotel, more so than my other northern properties. My arrival would mark the start of a full court, kitchen versus any department, basketball game. We played native style in bare feet. I was a corporate officer and highly respected, but never balked at living as the masses implored in times of joy. If I enjoyed my staff and the work was getting done, then it's all fun and games. I would join them for karaoke nights and beer gardens. I was always high on meth and I think some of them knew so, but treated me no differently because of that. They were just well rounded and aware, and mindful.

The resort I was responsible for was a well known commodity in that area of Davao as a wedding destination and shoreline photo venue. It was resort style with a long dock and a small family restaurant operated by the hotel at the very end of the dock, which was almost the length of a football field.

The former mayor of Davao, Rodrigo Duterte, and current Vice President and daughter, Sara Duterte, would frequent my resort. I had the pleasure in shaking hands with the former mayor and his family. They, the Dutertes, have given the country hope in its epic battle against drugs, mainly methamphetamines. The father and daughter tandem, famous for the implementation of martial law, have flown under the global household's radar in their power of example as far as how governments should operate. His campaign slogan is widely known around the country; "if you have drugs, you die today!" Rodrigo began executing drug dealers and addicts in the largest city, by land mass, in the world. Davao, Philippines.

Rodrigo Duterte would be sentenced to death after imprisonment in the United States for such cruel punishments, as we love playing the hero to global crises we caused. But, wouldn't it immediately fix almost every problem this country has? Jails would be 80% less full, taxes would be less than 15% on our highest earnings threshold, money would be expendable, jobs would be careening into the lowest unemployment level this country ever saw, and state funding would be relegated to tolls only. Trillions of dollars would be flushed healthily back into our schools and communities. Families and groups would build stronger bonds and trust more freely. Emotions would be authentic; people would be authentic. We would stop damning our own brothers and sisters for crimes they can't avoid. Life would revert to purity.

The United Nations and NATO have kept a close eye on President Duterte, yet they maintain his vision of a new world for Filipinos. They oppose his tactics, but keep their distance, for the world knows the feeble situation of Manila, spreading like wildfire through a poverty-stricken culture. A culture demoralized and compromised by one man, rebuilt by one other. Several of our world leaders have tried to interject with compassion, but Duterte knows they haven't walked a day on his streets. He has put drug users and dealers on watch. He has given his own citizens the authority to take matters into their own hands. The country surely has to take accountability for their situation, but it's only through the methods of extrajudicial killings and complete drug eradication that the Philippines will ever have a chance again.

If you were to take the time and sit in court for a day and listen to the public hearings, you would hear drugs and alcohol mentioned in almost every case. All correctional facilities would be noticeably less full, and all low-income communities would immediately start to develop. America would start to see its full potential. Confidence would be more infectious than COVID. Employment would be immediately rising to all-time highs. If the fear of death by firing squad within the current 24-hour frame doesn't change your perspective, then we can simply chalk it up to natural selection. In the Philippines, this man is God. If you're wondering why Mr. Duterte has stepped down from his mayoral office, it's because he stepped up. He is currently serving as the former 16th President of the Philippines. His tactics were so well received in cleaning up the largest city by land mass in the world, that he was elected in 2016. He served until June of 2022, where he would have been unanimously re-elected, except due to his Party designation he can serve only one term. His daughter, Sara, is patiently waiting to be elected into his role, and currently serving as Vice President while maintaining her fathers' fight. He, Duterte, single-handedly has given a country, overrun with drugs and squatters, a fighting chance. One could argue how sad it is to have let it get to that point, but you don't typically know where you're headed without direction until you're there. That's where we as a nation are failing and heading faster than people think. We put our hopes in recovery. The best thing that ever happened to my life as an addict was getting peeled off my comfortable bed in my parents' house at 40 years old, and

145

thrown right out the door. Pure, uncontested love is doing the hardest thing for yourself in order to help another. I knew they loved me, and I knew they let me walk all over them for years. My addiction laughed at their gullible stance and accepting ways. He, 'the other guy' in me used them, and put me in an uphill battle to get them back. There is victory out there, but it's built on tough love. I will give you one guess as to which one of our 195 known countries attempted to quell the violent tactics towards the Earth's scum. Yep, America! President Barrack Obama arranged a meeting to discuss Duterte's extrajudicial killings, then abruptly cancelled after Duterte called our former president the "son of a whore."

Keep in mind, while again this may sound hypocritical, if drugs were eradicated long before I was born, while they were growing out of control, we wouldn't be having this conversation. The fact is that I hate myself as an addict. I don't think anyone who uses drugs is necessarily bad, at all. I do believe it's time to show the world some tough love and put our foot down where we should've done long ago. Hindsight being irrefutable and unchanging, the only thing left to do that we haven't tried yet is brute force. I understand the alarming spike that would be created in motherless and fatherless families and the massive toll it will take on our nation's history, but in 30 years the world will have forgotten all about those families and friends they lost to the war on drugs. It would be a world built on authenticity of character and purity.

Desperate times call for desperate measures. When liabilities have all the boxes checked, our lawmakers have no desperation to act upon. No parents of the deceased will come clamoring for justice when no lives are lost. We're essentially damning the addicted to at least two years of court ordered programs. Most of these struggling addicts have children that are now displaced as they struggle with probates in custody battles for their own child. It's true that they're lacking the ability to care for that child, but if drugs weren't an option… would we be having this discussion?

Keep in mind I have zero interest in politics. This is merely an observation into philanthropy. If the fear of God doesn't wallop humans back into conformity and decency, I bet death will. Most governments are deeply entwined in nepotistic values and unnecessary, overpaid assignments, anyway. It simplifies a trillion-dollar problem. There is always an agenda in politics. How many laws are made in this country in response to a horrific, one-off accident? Rebecca, Amber, Adam, Andy, Vicky, Andre, Brady, Brett, Leandra, Jonathan, Jessica, Coogan, Amy, Caylee, Mann, Bland-Alison, Hatch, Meghan, Sami, Reagan, and Ryan White, to name just a few. All these laws are, I believe, while well intended in creating a solution, have only exacerbated a problem, while covering up any liability their position may have held. These laws are seen as reactive, not responsive. Reactive to pushback from grievances and those grieving. Reactive to people going through rigorous pain and loss. Reactive to emotion. Reactive is never going to be anything more than unstable. It's not to say that the laws, with respect to the victims, don't have merit. It's to point out the reactive nature to our nations problems, as opposed to a preemptive, responsive, lucid, well thought out plan of implementation. Oh, and, there are laws in place that speak to some of these namesake laws already, but the people aren't emotionally moved by a politician reminding them to stay one car length behind a car for every ten miles-per-hour you are traveling.

A response is something we can put some consideration to. Firm or fluffy, there are many forms of response, but only one reaction.... our reaction is the opposite, more often than not, than our response. Our response, as behavioral science would suggest, is simply our personal conclusion and decision towards the best outcome versus the least involvement, engagement, or effort, for most. This wasn't always the way our species thought. The optimal result was once a natural inclination for us humans, regardless of the physical or financial obligation.

My interest is in people, all people. People like me that haven't had the opportunities to recover. People like me that have practiced restraint through their using, but know they can't hold on forever. People with golden intentions and the desire and willingness to do whatever is necessary. People whose pain and shame have made them desperate. People with nothing to lose. Those are my people.

Those are the people strong enough to make the best decision for all. Those are the people that won't rely on claiming success by avoiding sensitive subject matter and dancing around the words *I was wrong*. Those are the people we need. Most of our lawmakers wouldn't know what a low-income housing project looks like, or had to split an Uber by combining all of their life savings just to get to tomorrow, where another battle lies ahead for a struggling, defeated addict. People who over-execute their well-aimed intentions. People who bleed and people who sweat. People that know how thin and long a rope it is, and don't balk at the work ahead. People who know the worldly benefit of a painful, yet, right decision. People who have accepted life as a perpetual challenge, not only for themselves, but for everyone they love and that loves them back.

Humans typically only respond when the fight comes to their backyard. Our politicians don't have to apply for EBT or government aid. They haven't had the pleasure of sleeping with furniture against the door, or behind their own bed with a dummy under the covers and a gun by their hip. They haven't lived in low income, drug infested environments. They haven't picked up their buddy at a trap house or given Narcan to a girlfriend that overdid her dose. They haven't stood in the cold for a bus or train, nor have they sized up a public building for a door to pry open and avoid the fatal cold and steal some warmth on a freezing night. They haven't experienced life like most people. Four out of 5 Americans live week to week, if they're lucky... We are way behind the global standards in elementary academics and are one of very few First World Nations not to offer their indigents a monetary stipend from the beginning of COVID through the finality, where and when at least 70% of all nationals became fully vaccinated (which means nothing). How can our lawmakers be making laws that will make a difference when they can't see there's any difference than what takes place in their version of normal, 1%-er life. Anyone, any goddamn person on fucking Earth understands that we can't visualize or encapsulate the level of defeat in someone else, and we can't fix a problem we can't see.

Rodrigo Duterte, shortly after elected, announced his proudest accomplishment as a leader. He announced his number of ordered executions of drug dealers and drug users and does so daily. He is a hardened man, but a man willing to be the bad guy for the future of his country. He relays his statistics daily to his people to remind them of conformity in a serious matter. A grave matter. He has said himself he will expedite his homeland's uncontrolled drug epidemic within his own actions and integrity. He's not waiting for the pumpkin to turn into road kill. He's forcing Cinderella back into her proverbial glass slipper. Turning the country on its head for the greater good.

No one set of values or lifestyles is one hundred percent good, nor one hundred percent bad. There is always, even in the most pure souls, a modicum of darkness. It's the cosmic balance and our fate as humans. Duterte is, without question, reactive to his crisis but he is aware of his haste. He questions the indifference of those that won't stand and fight beside him. I question indifference, always.

His original declaration of martial law was following a radical's bomb going off in Davao in 2014, a few short years after I lived there. I realized shortly after getting clean that time around, after leaving the Philippines, just how close to death I was; traveling the streets in Davao with a pocketful of drugs, thinking I was untouchable. Duterte didn't start this war for riches, or personal gain, and not for worldwide notoriety, but for the health and safety of the greater mass, those that value life beyond substance, and his fellow Filipinos. He has declared over 31,000 executions as of early 2022, since he took office as President, and has an even larger number of executions when totaling in the lives lost during his, and his daughter's, incumbency in Mindinao.

Rodrigo Duterte risks his life every minute of every day. While many of you may not empathize with his situation, know this; he has no financial investments in the war on drugs. He's not a recovering addict. He's not a monster nor a Saint. He's not living lavishly and basking in his riches. He's not even widely liked, socially. He maintains that in spite of his opposition he upholds his nation's chair in the United Nations as he maintains his respect for foreign diplomacy on a case-by-case basis.

Duterte never questioned what the time frame would be until his country sees itself crawl from the ashes it currently resides in, only that the job was non-negotiably imminent, and he was the head of the campaign. He still is the global leader in the drug war, a war more and more countries are failing in their fights, our own included. There is obviously a massive social impact from any execution or life abruptly ended, but the tolerance and opportunity we provide the constitutionally incapable are taxing the benevolent communities, thus, tipping

the scales of potential balance. The full potential of our species

will never be met until we forcefully remove the problem.

Drugs are, undoubtedly, our greatest challenge as a species. It's

never an easy decision to end a human life, but the time for

redemption has passed, and it's time to build a truly better

tomorrow. It's ruthless and inhumane in itself, I get it. It

contradicts everything I've spent my time and every effort into,

sobriety. I get that, too. I think it's safe to say the only safe way,

is no way. We lost. Drugs won! Just ask an addict in recovery.

Someone on the right path has this acceptance. I wouldn't

expect the unaffected to do anything more than revolt and

laugh, but the only way to attack any issue, is head on; clearly

navigating the immediate necessities and most crime friendly

neighborhoods in the country. Sometimes all it takes is an

example to set things in motion. I'm willing to lose a few good

men to the cause, even myself, should I relapse.

If you were to read into his character, or watch President Duterte address the nation, he is unapologetically cold, because he knows the war on drugs is far from over. He has done what no other man could or would do… be the villain his people need him to be.

6 | Fatherhood

From this moment on, until the end of me, there are no more splits on the train track of my life. There are no more diversions or alternatives. No more audibles or trick plays. No more time wasted on things I know will never work out. And, until the day actually came where I finally accepted that the only enemy I had on this Earth was myself, I could never really patch up the main artery my problems flowed from. I was frantically exacerbating all my issues by trying to Band-Aid each symptom of the main problem, my addiction. That doesn't necessarily mean my physical body being high from narcotics, so much as it means an addicted headspace. A toxic system of logic. Just because I put down drugs, or didn't for that matter, it's the ultimate acceptance of me as a person that I struggled with. Mostly through guilt in using, or shortcomings as a father, my problem exists even when the drugs aren't in my system. It's the self-seeking, reactive part of my character. The voice inside me that urges me to take, take, take! Just as it does for every other addicted mind on Earth. I'm far from unique and finally able to accept that. That's where having a child may have pushed me ahead a little faster than my disease anticipated. My disease, without question, had my last vision of life as I was living it, a short way away and expiration quickly approaching, all the while telling me he's got things under control. He's a fucking liar and definitely male. The thought of using drugs enters my mind almost daily, even after years of recovery, but the person in my head that calls the shots today is the guy I thought I was…. or wanted to be for a long time. The addicted version of myself, "the other guy," as I've named him, created a reality that wasn't visceral or attainable. He's ensured me during every run that we would come out on top, ahead of the others out there. He promised me financial and emotional success while leeching off the chemicals that create that success. He's planned the most exciting adventures for us while keeping me in my own home with blinds drawn to protect us from the outside noise and paranoia he was causing. He gaslights and abuses, mentally and physically. He polluted everything about the authentic version of me, of life.

The days are gone that I have to wake up and beat myself with an emotional tool disguised in self-pity. The years are gone where I have to look back with disappointment in myself having not done or achieved what I had planned. The days of unrealistic planning and dreaming are gone, as I have laid them to rest with my sober mind. The decades behind me are ones I can't fix or take a mulligan on, but I can aspire towards penance on a moment by moment understanding that **now** is the only moment that will clear that shame and guilt. The days, months, or years ahead will be shaped by my success in staying present in my current moment, even the one I'm typing now. Shame and pain are inevitable, but suffering is optional. This is what I've come to accept as full-fledged reality…. finally. The days ahead are marked by my title as a father, son, brother, and partner, not as a recovering addict, although that will never go away. That is **my** battle to fight and one that will never seep into the efforts of another human I love…again.

I received an education in the halls of Alcoholics Anonymous, and then tried applying each of my new, practiced set of values out in the real world. For some of us it works, and for others, it doesn't. For me, initially it did. Once I got back out that door, I never got 'celebrated' the same. I felt like I was just another relapser. I wasn't the young kid anymore, bright and eager to help. I had shame, and that shame, for some addicts and alcoholics, becomes too heavy a cross to carry. I have been fortunate enough to make it this far, and actually consider myself being on borrowed time from here on out. It heightens the overall sense of gratitude and connection I have with my own life. The time I get with Evelyn, my daughter, is as far as I'm concerned, a giant, undeserved bonus. I have repeatedly pissed away opportunities a good man would never discard. She swears she needs me, but I'm more than certain I need her way more. I don't think she understands that, but I know it....and, those that have seen me through the tough times absolutely know it. That kid saved my life. I kept a blog for her while we were estranged. Over three years I funneled money into a bank for her, never letting my addiction ruin Evelyn's life. Mine, maybe... hers, not a chance. "The other guy" made his run for it, and almost never let me get back, but I did. Maybe it was the degree of difficulty where I earned this bonus, but I won't disrupt the plan life has for me, if this is it. Every day I had to wake up and see Evelyn, curled up with her cat, Loka, protecting her angelic little head. I would flash her lights, watch her squint, and peel out of bed, always with her arms outstretched for a hug. A moment we can remember forever. It was the way she felt safe to start her day. She stood, listlessly, but never discontent or bratty. She would wrap her gangly arms around my neck and give me a kiss as I brushed her ratty hair from tickling my chin to give her a kiss on her perfectly toned, olive-skinned forehead. As we would separate, physically, we would start to plan our day. She would remind me of my stuff just as much as I reminded her of hers. She would get herself ready to shower and catch the bus while I made her lunch. We walked Brady, our Great Pyrenees Dog, to the bus stop to see her off. She would always come kiss me in front of the other kids, something I hope never goes away, although age may defer my kisses to her first boyfriend, a day I've mentally prepared for over the course of her life. Evelyn, being of mixed race, is a pretty girl, and eventually going to be my biggest problem. She's my penance, and I would drop anything for her, and I did.

Less than six years ago, just after Evelyn's fourth birthday, we met each other for the first time that she would be able to remember, and it's been an intoxicating ride; physically and metaphorically ever since. First, I want to tell you what brought us here…

I grew up the middle child in a little place called "Mingya Valley," a quaint little junkyard of a neighborhood in the town of a city of Methuen, Massachusetts. I'm forty-three years old and currently residing in the same neighborhood, after spending most of my life in some meth addicted hellhole usually across the country or world. Don't get me wrong, my surroundings have always been beautiful, but my ability to enjoy them has always been regulated by my drug intake. Now it's dictated by my achievements as a father, son, brother, and uncle. My addicted self-drew his last breath some months ago. I'm sure many of you are focusing on the word months and shaking your heads, cautioning my words inside your own mind, and laughing at the exclamatory testament regarding my recovery. The point is, I know when I'm done, and I'm done! I'm not scared of life anymore. I have a kid that needs me to be clear. We tried to incorporate "the other guy" into our lives but cleaning up the mess he causes has run its course.

We, myself along with my brother and sister, would walk about a half a mile to our bus, cracking the fiberglass pieces from spark plugs and throwing them at windows of cars that hadn't been smashed yet, and watching the windows explode. It blew my mind. We would steal this cranky old bag's tomatoes from her garden and run for it. We would infiltrate farms and get chased by Mr. Bonano, who was rumored to blast his shotgun at trespassing kids. This was never proved nor did any children ever go missing at the time, but we believed it. I basically lived the life that you read in memes on social media from anyone posting from Generation X. I rode my bike, caught frogs, and came home muddy and broke my bones. I got poison ivy like a motherfucker. My brother and I would dress ourselves up in our hockey equipment when we started getting a rash and tie each other into bed with whatever remaining extremities we could still use. We did this so we wouldn't scratch the poison ivy, not realizing that the equipment itself would be scratching it and heating it up through the night. Ultimately, we were exacerbating the situation. Some calamine lotion, and at times, prednisone were my childhood friends, and they weren't imaginary.

My brother, an absolute rock of a man, was always my best friend and hero growing up. He always took a backseat to my incessant need for attention. He played the role of big brother to perfection. Anywhere we went outside it would be together. We would have Whiffleball tournaments in the backyard and set up NHL '93 on Super Nintendo in our backyard shed so we wouldn't disturb my parents during the day while we were playing it like fiends, and they were trying to catch a nap between their double shifts that each of them was working so that we could all get braces and go to private schools. It's not as if the valley was a terrible place to live, but my parents were raised in the projects, and they were determined to never let us live that life. The valley was lower blue collar, and that was a step up. Little did they know that by enabling my using for decades they helped me finally achieve their childhood success; life on the streets and projects. A life they saw inconceivable shame in. A life I ended up living and escaping.

My brother and I recruited anyone within a two-mile bicycle ride to our home for tournaments of all kinds. We played street hockey until we couldn't see the ball rolling across the worn down, weather eroded, hot top pavement anymore...on nights we didn't have some practice or religious studies. My parents lived the lives of hockey parents, with my little sister, Melissa, doing figure skating. It's no wonder my first car was a Zamboni! My father used to love coming to watch me play; hockey and baseball... I was out there for blood, and I can't fucking stand losing. I'm the most disgraceful loser and winner. I have this nasty competitive human that lives inside me, and my father reveled in it. He was always a fairly good athlete growing up, but in my town I was the first pick in the draft for baseball every year and I was the first line right wing on any hockey team I played on. I went on to be an all-conference hockey player in high school, but by that point, drugs had started to make themselves a priority in my life. The day my father took me off his pedestal was the day he first knew I smoke pot. Twenty-eight years later and our relationship is still rebuilding. A couple good runs of sobriety gave him hope, but epic relapses and ugly circumstances, all surrounding me, have helped me position myself with a daunting uphill fight decades later. A fight I'm finally up for. My father is the only human who had the balls to show me the tough love that it took for me to see... fatherhood is the most amazing gift in this world.

Despite our differences, I can see without reservation, that if I were half the father my dad is, and has been his whole life, I would be perfectly happy with my efforts as one myself. On days when I was pitching for my baseball team, and he knew how nervous he made me by sitting in the three rows of metal bleachers in a sun-soaked field while hollering sporadic reminders about my mechanics, he would come to the game in a separate car and watch me from the woods, so he didn't make me nervous. My father, much like myself, expects a lot out of his people, but my father would never be a burden. He never weighed me down…. he lifted me up. He would make sure I had no excuse if I didn't pitch well. He's the only man who's held me accountable in this world to date. We both follow the mindset that; it's not too much to ask to just be fucking normal, or normal as we knew it. We despise laziness. We immediately judge those who take short cuts. We measure effort. Not the effort that you give, but the potential of your effort, then the effort forward. Time and logic fix anything, and there's really nothing on Earth worth getting worked up about it. He executes the latter statement way more maturely than I can, but I understand the value in it.

Having had grown up in housing projects in Lawrence, MA, and met there when they were kids, my mother and father knew the importance of giving us a better life. They kept us away from the hustle that they grew up in. Once I became a professional scumbag, I understood why. Hockey, when I was young and living in New England, was an elitist sport. Skates alone were about $300. Today a good set of hockey skates, which will be grown out of if you are still growing, as we were, will run you over $1000. My mother has worked for a single company her entire life soldering chipboards, while my father has worked in textile mills running Polartec fabrics for over 40 years. He supplemented his income by managing low income housing units and driving a school bus to get a break on our tuition. My father is the example of humility any human should aspire towards, irrefutably the highest level of natural integrity of any human I have had the pleasure of knowing.

My father, in stark contrast to my myself and my speckled existence, has never even piqued his curiosity when it comes to inhaling a cigarette or dabbling in narcotics. He's never tried either. While I struggled to get clean in my early twenties, my father was unapologetically deaf when it came to listening to anything regarding addiction as a disease. While I concur that it is a disease, and I concur the cure, at least for me, is tough love. His ignorance or lack of understanding at my inability to stop ultimately made us distant as the years, and my disease, careened on. Not that our reconciliation was contingent upon him recognizing addiction as a disease, but it helps expedite our relationship as father and son again. He had always maintained that I was just running amok and enjoying my drugs and hoes, selfishly, not knowing that I was dying a slow death, emotionally and physically, every second of every minute. He sees the efforts in me today. He sees the pain more so than the efforts. He knows I would never put myself through that sort of pain. He knows how much I love being a father myself. He gets as excited as a guy like him gets when he recognizes the amount of love and connection Evelyn and I have established. He remembers the days when she was a stranger to us…to me.

His tone in watching me fail repeatedly in my sobriety and fatherhood had changed from *just stop* to *I wish I could help you more, Matthew!"* Neither of us are men of empathy, but that was enough for me to know he loves me. I'm not sure my dad will ever mouth those words. The only time I saw him cry was when we had to put our dog, Kobe, down. Kobe was the dog my father never wanted and fell so deeply in love with. Kobe's life brought new meaning to the phrase frisbee genocide. Actually, that's not a known phrase by any language standard, but it certainly applies to Kobe! His life's purpose was not what I saw in that movie about the dogs, but one laced with a short stack of frisbees between his disgusting jowls while he gyrated like a broken washing machine. He was mentally addicted to frisbees. In full honesty and transparency, my father very well may have caught his first understanding and sense of empathy towards addicts through watching Kobe. He followed my father anywhere, unless there was a frisbee involved. His allegiances 1.) frisbee, 2.) my dad, 3.) anything else. On one of my parents' weekly summer rentals on the seacoast of New Hampshire one summer, Kobe's frisbee got caught in the undertow, and he refused to leave the water, circling around like a shark circling his prey, for over 45 minutes before my parents had to perform

a search and rescue. I'm not sure Kobe ever got over that

frisbee, but he would've given his life for it. Kobe's death was

the only day I saw my father shed a tear in his entire life, like I

said. I never expected to be like him, seeing I was a total

mama's boy, and have shed enough tears for the two of us.

My father was the youngest of seven. All his four brothers and

his two sisters born before him were alcoholics and drug

addicts. I never thought about any of them that way until I was

an adult and realized they all had chronic substance issues. I was

always a little wet behind the ears when I was younger. They

owned bars and kept books. They shuffled illegal gambling

machines in and out of our shed when police were doing stings.

They were always up to something, something not legal, or

good. My father was the only one of his family to take a stand against drugs and embark on a life he envisioned when he met my mother, a pothead, and the only girl and youngest of four. Her older brothers suffered from the same grave affliction as my father's siblings, alcoholism. Her eldest brother, Kenny, my godfather, is non-active in his alcoholism, and, thus, a pretty decent guy. My father doesn't relate to anyone that uses. His shame in me during my teens and early twenties was noticeable to say the least. I'll never forget the day the movers stumbled across an old water bong my parents confiscated from my car and hid behind their dresser and asked my family in front of a small crowd what they were supposed to do regarding packing the bong. The embarrassment on my father's face spoke loudly enough for me to remember it 25 years later.

My brother Michael was always like steady-Eddie. Never too high or never too low. The consummate consistent professional. He weighed risk and acted accordingly. I was the complete contrast of a human, always seeking attention and having to be the loudest mouth in the room. My brother looked at me a lot like the way like my dad did. He was proud of me, regardless, but he, too, knows immediately how things are inside me. It's scary. My addiction has taken its toll on him as well. The fact that he's married to the biggest cunt I've ever met retards our process of reconnection a little more than I would like it to. My dad, however, would go through any amount of anguish to see the clean me succeed. Dad looks the other way and disengages immediately when he senses "the other guy" in the room. I feel it, too. My father and I rarely share the same opinion, but we don't have to agree with each other today. We can agree to disagree….and it's okay. Our issues have always been directly with and through my addiction. When I was about to head out for college, I had just turned the corner into regular using, be it coke or crack or ecstasy or pills or weed. I didn't need to know what things were when I took them, just how they made me feel. I was fortunate enough, or should say, have been fortunate enough, thus far, to have never injected narcotics into my bloodstream. I was never afraid of needles, just myself. I use everything like a slob and always have. I was an addict when I was three years old, seeing an eye doctor in Boston to cure my incessant blinking due to 24-hour Nintendo-itis. It got me young, and I always knew it, but somewhere just hoped I became less of a wrecking ball as life went on. Who knew I would have to work at it! Regardless of the way I injected drugs or didn't, my father couldn't give a fuck how I took them, just that I did. And, to him, that was an attack on the family.

By the time I was in my mid-thirties, I had experienced a couple multi-year bouts of sobriety. My father saw sobriety catapult my career and accolades. He frequented my restaurant, always proud of what I was serving. He would talk about me to every friend or frenemy that would listen. He loved the sober me more than anyone else could. His heart splits when he sees my eyes and catches "the other guy" looking back at him. I could almost hear the pain it caused.

'The other guy' is a predator, serial killer, pussy, coward, loser, and total weirdo. He fucks up the shit the normal me has working like clockwork. I invite him out when the normal me doesn't feel like being part of reality anymore. I don't know why I ever gave myself the thought that it was okay to bury my feelings in methamphetamines, but it definitely doesn't work (I did mention my track record in adult decision making). "The other guy" is born from that stuff. He's born from other stuff as well, like just about any morally deficient soul singeing exercise, but mostly drugs. "The other guy" starts to do my bidding when things get going too well, and when I am having a hard time finding anything wrong. We're both not sure how to handle success, but he's always up for the challenge of crumbling it overnight.

My father woke up every day of his life a power of example. It was probably why I was so nervous becoming one, because the sample I was trying to emulate was completely infallible. He was a rock, without fail, every moment of my life. He has never gone one unreturned phone call or text. Becoming a father, I weighed and measured myself against him, and I failed. It wasn't until recently that I accepted our differences, and became a pretty decent parent of my own, albeit maybe a minute too late. Evelyn will never feel anything but adoration and love for me and holds me on the same pedestal I held my dad on, so there's hope.

My first day being a dad I was high on meth, broke, and then locked by military police in a Philippine hospital where I had spent all the doctor's money on drugs and was barricaded in with Evelyn still swaddled; and, on the verge of complete collapse. It took less than one minute of Evelyn's life to commit an act far worse than anything I saw my dad do in 31 years of my life, until then. That is the irrevocable truth. This is where I take umbrage with members of Alcoholics Anonymous for imploring self-reconciliation and amendments to those I've wronged, including the wrongs I've done myself, to myself. If I would never forgive anyone else for something, I sure as hell am not forgiving myself for it. That's not to say I'm going to walk around and beat myself with the proverbial bat for the rest of my life. It just means I recognize the heinous nature of my actions as irreconcilable and move on creating the best **now** I can. I'd love to paint a prettier picture, but the truth isn't always pretty. The truth is the truth, regardless of euphemisms or compassion. The American MO rests in not divulging the truth with reality, but with a rose-colored brush of intentions and misdirection.

At the time Evelyn was born, I justified not having a nickel, but I knew it was my disease pacifying the real me. "The other guy" had stepped up and taken his shot at parenting and left nothing but a line of DCF letters and appointments, drug screens for dad, jail time, car crashes, absent nights, stiffed hookers banging on my door, and barren wastelands of habitats I chose to call 'home.' I lived like a tweaker and brought my own kid along for the ugly ride. This is where the AA forgive yourself bullshit gets me confused. I won't beat myself up over it, but I'm not giving myself a hall pass on it either. I will remember every shitty moment I had as a father. That is what helps me to not forget them. That is not something I would forgive someone forever doing to me, so I won't pretend to have found my inner peace. Inner peace is day-to-day, moment-to-moment, a series of successive moments leading to the culmination of **now,** the only relevance to life.

Evelyn and I have struggled to be with each other since the start. It's a battle we're currently on the losing end of, but we never stop fighting. Last August, after her tenth birthday, I saw her off at Logan airport in Boston for a one month, post COVID visit to see her mom, before she started fifth grade. She never returned. Evelyn had always dreamed of living with me since we had reunited after I finally got my shit together and showed up, but her mother was always a stalwart and more interested in her own happiness than that of Evelyn's. When a tuition payment, and another…were missed in 2017 at Evelyn's school, her mother had no choice but to send her to live with me. The trip to see her mom ended with an abduction. Evelyn made sure her mom, Annie, had full understanding of her position and decision. At age eight, Evelyn was allowed to come live with me. We kept close to Annie over the two plus years she was here, most of which I struggled through, as I had relapsed after a relationship ended in an unacceptable abortion. I was relieved to have everything in order for Evelyn's arrival; balanced work schedules and enough time to whisk Evelyn off to every play, practice, and pottery class she was enrolled in, which was every night, except Monday, when we would have movie night. We became inseparable almost instantly.

At the end of Evelyn's vacation, her unused ticket and empty seat were another obvious symptom of failed parenthood, from the two people Evelyn should be able to put her unequivocal faith into, mom and dad. Emirates Airlines called me in a panic, as they were expecting to chaperone Evelyn back to me in Boston, as we had become so accustomed to doing over the years since we had reunited. They said Evelyn never arrived for her check-in. Having just had direct communication with her via a Messenger call, I reached out to Annie via Facebook to see what was going on…. her response was the first words in my life that shifted every ounce of anger and hate onto one person, Annie.

Eve not going back to US. Maybe in a couple years can talk again. - Annie punched in her chat box. *(Evelyn hates being called Eve)*

Those words were the line in the sand. That was the day I stopped pretending to be on board with forgiveness. That was where humanity tipped the scales for me. Granted, one human could and should never be the source of ardent fact regarding a species, as a whole, but the culmination of compassion-less attempts at self-preservation by people across the globe, infected throughout every border, was unsought validation of true evil on Earth, for me…. self-will run riot.

I was airborne and on my way to Thailand as fast as our government could process my documents…. almost two months later, only to have our exit plan uncovered by Annie. It's not easy getting a 10yr old to hide her passports from a crazy lady in a one-bedroom shophouse. I'm now home, awaiting our day in court for Evelyn to come home, but it leaves me with the opportunity to reset, to build off the success

I had as a dad, and apply it in my life without Evelyn. It's worked. I wake up reminding myself that my kid is out there, waiting for me to rescue her, and I keep that fire burning throughout the day, every day. That's why I say she saved my life. She has without knowing it. I won't be as pious as to say I'm cured of my disease, because I know the dangerousness in my twenty-five years of watching life through "the other guys'" eyes. I know myself, and I knew every time I ever got clean or used, or repeated the cycle, that my life was definitely going to cross that path again, and it did. I always challenged myself how long I could go without my drug, always falling far short of my projection. This is the infinite battle in knowing myself. The number of times I repeated a destructive cycle. All the times I promised myself and my family I was done. I wouldn't buy my self-peddled bullshit either. I know I'm done. Even on payday, when my daughter is unreachable and abducted, and a three-hour drive lies ahead for me to earn my forty five thousand dollars a year, I am content. It's a full life, and there are so many gifts of sobriety in the previous statement, writing it almost makes me teary. Maybe I'm projecting my failed attempts at fatherhood into farming, but it's worth it. There's not a single beating heart in my home that outranks another. All the animals, minus the feline's obsession with my sugar glider, Spidey, are cohabitating perfectly. The squeaky wheel gets the grease in this house, and I try to never be the squeaky wheel. Never operating perfectly, but never with angst or frustration, or chaos. They, my animals, are a source of placidity and serenity. Evelyn loves them all, too. She would give every second of her time for anyone or anything of need. She's the only thing on this fucked up earth I have done right. I've always enjoyed my animals, and they have given me more than I could ever give them. We bond. Evelyn bonds. We use our time with the animals, and together, to align ourselves in honesty and openness. She's free to be who she wants, how she wants. At 10 years old, and a shit load of life experience, Evelyn has displayed enough good decision-making for her to have earned it. I didn't make consecutive good decisions until I was in my late thirties.

It wasn't until I gave in completely to a life of parenting that I could be happy just squeaking by. I was used to being a martyr for my job, and travel the world opening up posh Beach clubs, boutique resorts, and exotic fine dining venues throughout Southeast Asia. Being a father, has an always will be, the one job I have in life that I'd like to perfect. I have accepted my flaws and past miscues, and I don't let that dictate who I am today. I understand we all start at different points, and having lived a life of privileged, it's few and far between the times I've had to start behind the eight ball. What may seem like a small task to some, is monumental for a guy like me. In Evelyn's absence, I've maintained my role in life as a father, I sought work that would

never interfere with Evelyn's schedule and still pays me enough

to support our lives and set aside time with her. I have all her

appointments and childhood protocols scheduled in my mind. I

know when the PTA meetings are, and I volunteer for

Halloween nights, and school dances. I don't need to let my

mind convince me I'm a bad person, and relive the nights I

wasn't home, while Evelyn laid in bed, riddled with anxiety over

when I would come home. I spent the first two years slack-

jawed, nervous, scared, and ultimately, high. All because I was

afraid of my eight-year-old child. I was afraid to fail so bad, that

I numbed myself. How do you open the door to your eight-

year-olds' bedroom and let them know that you're not qualified

to be their parent? The thought actually crossed my mind the

nights I laid shaking, crying over the person I was, and more

importantly, the parent I was. None of the aforementioned

gives me any excuse to be the way I was. No feeling on earth should ever change an action. The next moment and the only moment I'll ever have the opportunity to make better is **now.** If I maintain the practice of being engaged, attentive, and honest in every moment that features me, I will never need a drug again. I will never need to worry if I'm different or doing things right. I'll be in the moment....my moment, and those negative, drug filled thoughts are symptoms of my soul escaping the moment, placing a feeling of expectation on it, and acting out with entitlement. I'm expecting nothing more than to have that next moment to do my best with. Sure, I'll fail way more often than I succeed, but I will be me. That is more than anyone with a micro-newton of energy could say. I think one of the saddest lives anyone could live is one of irrelevance. Not to be noticed, to be of service to another person. To help someone's life in a way that they could never do for themselves. To me, that's where the purest forms of happiness in my life come from. They don't come from my accolades as a chef, or my bank account, or whatever I'd like to fill my head with, that makes me think I'm someone important. I honestly believe that our output of mindfulness and gratitude and love will dictate our core sensation.

The only part of me that isn't my daughter's father is "the other guy." Since he's retired, it's the first time in my life I've actually had the opportunity to enjoy my sobriety on my terms. Prior to now, everything has been on the terms of Alcoholics Anonymous, constantly threatening and keeping a watchful eye. I'm sure by now you've picked up on stubbornness and pride, so just bear with me. The program works, and it works for me, but the rest of my life doesn't work for me, in AA. The situation being so sensitive with Evelyn, kidnapped and in the clutches of the evil, psychotic woman she calls *mommy*. Suffocated by the afflicted and lawfully bound to her on Thai soil. Munchhausen by proxy is my guess at what's wrong with her mother.

Integrity, one of my favorite words, was taught to me by my late clinician at Spring Hill. He was one of the only guys on this Earth I would ever think had no chance of going back out there to the streets, where he suffered innumerable attempts at failed sobriety. Shortly after I left Spring Hill, Andy, that alpha dog clinician, passed away from a heroin overdose. He relapsed after they sold the facility and hired all new clinicians, and he was left without a job, thus, going back to his drug of choice. He had given his brother a call and told him he was going to take one last dose, pleading with his brother to come pick him up and take him to a detox. By the time his brother got there, Andy was dead on the scene.

Once we lose our connection to the real world, it gets pretty tough. There's no place to hide from "the other guy." Goes to show what I know. Andy, however, left me with an especially important piece of advice. The remarkably simple phrase that "integrity is who you are when people aren't watching."

Well, I won't get into my entire dissertation on religion, but know that I am more than certain of a cosmic system of weights and balances that measures our, us human's, integrity and issues our fate accordingly. I know that if I were to relapse between now and the next time I see Evelyn, whenever that is, there will be no happy ending for me. There will be shocked disappointment at losing. I did mention how I felt about losing. Evelyn, having been parent kidnapped going on six months now, hasn't seen my efforts but I know someone has. Someone or something... but I know right action breeds right consequences. And if it doesn't, then I just keep trying. I don't and won't stop until that kid is happy and back home. The only thing that will stop me is methamphetamines, and that has always been the way, but never again. Evelyn's happiness and life are my methamphetamines now.

You tell me how many walls would be needed to hold you back? Here is an unprovoked writing in my daughter's journal. There would never be a day I would cross the threshold of decency towards my daughter and violate her personal space, but this page coincidentally was written in my work notebook…a book I hadn't needed since COVID began.

Evelyn Mali Garon

English Assignment

05/09/2021

Title: My Dad

My Dad is a great person because he makes everyone laugh. His also really smart and talented. He is really fun to hang out with. He will also help anyone. He is also very trustworthy so he will never go back on his words. He will never hide anything from you. I re look up to him because I really want to have these character traits when I'm older.

That was the last thing she wrote me before she left on that plane. Still stings a bit.

The quintessential boundary that my integrity is no longer allowed to breach is using drugs. There are no more lives left for this sly cat. What is life less purpose? Existence. Existence is an idle word, and the last thing I want in my life is to have done nothing but occupy land mass and consume endless entitlements that someone, some anticipation filled bloke misinformed me of. I think on my own two feet…. big congrats to me, I know. I'll pass on the trophy. Some days reap a plentiful bounty of knowledge and healthy dialogue, and some days I sound like I should be wearing a helmet and licking windows. It's hit or miss, but that's that risky fence I love to ride. I don't refute anything, as I implored earlier, but the head banging art of expectation and predetermined protocols of anticipation are no longer in my itinerary. I live in this very moment, and focus all my energy there, thus, relinquishing the opportunity to get lost in days past, or days yet to come, should fortune favor the chronically wrong and unprepared.

7 | Everything

There's a certain and describable feeling to opening your eyes in the morning knowing that you have had a clear memory to your last drawn breath before bed and the less than distant acknowledgement of the contentment in that thought alone. Then the next few movements feel just as fresh; the body and mind are on the same page. That is one of the most overlooked catalysts for surviving another 1440 minutes.

March 3, 2022, 6:40 PM - The eleventh anniversary to my daughter's birth... to the minute. It's been six months since she's been kidnapped by her mother and retained for no other reason than her mothers' pride and stubbornness. I received a text from my mom saying she's gotten word from Annie, Evelyn's mother, that will allow them to speak via video call at 7 PM. It's the most fearful moment I've had in quite some time. The last time we had spoken was on November 12th at a police station in Bangkok, where Evelyn pleaded and cried to police for her release and return to the United States only to be met with fierce opposition and negligence. Police stated that the mother has 51% control in Thailand when, come to find out, that is not actually true. We left that day with the police order stating that although she would not be coming home with me to the United States where she excels in every area of life, we would have two days to see each other on the last two days of my visit to Thailand, November 19th and 20th, 2021. Being nervous at her mother's mental instability, I placed an AirTag (tracking device) on Evelyn to track her whereabouts. It's what's allowed me to find her in the first place after sending her back to see her mother for what was supposed to be a one month vacation before returning to Boston to start fifth grade. Her AirTag the following morning was seen five hundred miles away near Laos and Cambodia. Her mother vanished at the very thought of me being nearby and my daughter wanted nothing more than to be with me. Returning to the police station was a three hour ordeal that culminated in the phrase "this is a matter for child and family court." Try taking that one in the ass!

This girl of mine has endured the most arduous emotional pain that I've seen a 10 year old go through without physical violence or death being a factor. She was ripped out of her life unapologetically by a woman who has nothing to offer her. A woman she never once asked to call in over two years of living with me. A woman who has no influence in her life. A clown. A woman so clouded by her own insecurities and inadequacies that she would tear the life apart of her eldest daughter. Maybe the fact that her other daughter (not mine) has a severe mental illness has something to do with it, I just can't be sure. What I am sure of is that Evelyn has no desire to be where she is and is doing the best fucking job she can. Day in and day out, this girl is unflinchingly strong in her ability to adapt to her environment.

When I hear the news of the call, knowing that my own request to speak to my daughter on her birthday and every day since that day in November have gone unanswered, I let my parents know I'd be there. We all know that this is probably the last time we're going to speak to her, seeing as her mother is making every effort to make sure that Evelyn has no recollection of who I am, and would interpret my inclusion to the call as a breach in trust. What she doesn't understand is the amount of love and connection we, Evelyn and I, have for each other. That is undeniable.

Annie is interested in flaunting her mixed baby around Bangkok exclaiming how mature and polished she's become. She doesn't speak more than ten words in a day to Evelyn. She takes her phone, the one I paid for, before sending Evelyn on her twilight zone-ish vacation some six months ago, and blocks any communication between parties that aren't approved. I currently am on the unapproved list, to my daughter's anguish.

Annie has an inclination towards deceit. It wasn't like I was unable to pick up on this in my time living with her and in Thailand, but to impose it in a way that affects the happiness of your own child is something I will never come to grips with. It's something I will never understand nor do I want to. Thai culture, as beautiful as it is, relies on the importance of fabricating the truth in any situation to ease the inner turmoil of those manipulated, but most importantly to ease their own inner demons. What you don't know won't hurt you is the basic belief in Thailand. Evelyn knows this and she knows the importance of the truth.

As we're all sitting in the living room in anticipation of Evelyn to call, we discuss tactic. I will remain out of sight so as to not disrupt the time my parents and brother and his children get to spend with Evelyn. And knowing Annie… we can pretty much all agree that this is going to be the last call before the trial. It's Evelyn's birthday and certainly not a call we're going to omit for the sake of Annie's feelings.

March 3rd, 2022, 7:01PM – The call comes in to my mother's phone and I see Evelyn on the other end. It's the first glimpse I've had of the best part of me in over three months, when we were sprinting for our lives in a Bangkok compound and being told false promises about our reunion.

I'm hiding around a corner but I can hear the monotony in Evelyn's tone. She's bored as usual in Bangkok, melancholy at best. Her discomfort fills the room as it's clear she's searching for words that don't upset her mother, who is standing right behind her, monitoring every word. She is still not in school, claiming that her teacher has caught COVID. Last I heard she wasn't enrolled in school anyway. This is maddening for Evelyn as her connection to her peers is the greatest source of her happiness, besides the one she shares with me. As each of my family members take turns saying happy birthday and singing the birthday song, I appear from around the corner. I see Evelyn 's eyes shift toward me; she bursts out in tears. Her hair is ratty and discolored, her forehead riddled with acne, and her face says enough to know that the three months spent blocking my existence from her life has had a reverse effect. Evelyn is still my little soldier and the most connected part of my soul.

Last time we saw each other on US soil; saying goodbye at the gate of JFK airport, we had just one dog and one cat. I'm up to seventeen animals now, and Evelyn feels the energy they bring to life back here, her rightful home. I feel her heart tear over not being able to hug me, and she certainly knows how mine is bleeding. She sees my two silver labradors sprinting around the living room and her cousin James in his onesie pajamas trying to say her name...he's only two, but keeps a vivid connection to Evelyn even though she's been absent for half his life. Olivia, her five-year-old cousin and Jame's older sister, is trying to do handstands and show Evelyn all the tricks she's learned during her abduction. My parents look at me with tears in their eyes because they just realized once again how unmovable we are. Evelyn is fixed on finding my voice. It's an uneasy feeling for her, and one that will surely put a damper on her eleventh birthday. For that one moment, before Annie has a chance to slam down the call, I'm connected again... we're connected again. I hurriedly let Evelyn know that I'll be arriving in Bangkok on April 20th and reaffirm her that there isn't a day that goes by, not a fucking minute that goes by that she isn't in the number one spot in my life. *See you in April baby girl, let's get that pretty face home!* The call ends abruptly.

Most of the feelings running through me for the past six months have been anger, but I like to term it as 'lucid desperation.' A clarity in my mind with an acute sense of direction and no room for error or defeat. It's a silent rage, but one that seems to flow through me with inexplicable clarity and mindfulness. Evelyn is my sole purpose. There is only one path and I don't fucking care how many times I have to say that. Sometimes I'm convincing myself, but I don't get off that goddamn path. It's like a burning fucking locomotive careening right on the track, heading exactly where it's supposed to go… into the heart of that little girl, to bring her back home. At any other juncture in my life when this sort of emotional strife become unavoidable, I turned to drugs. I would singe my brain with meth and indifference. The thought and the desire are gone. Gone, gone. My addiction is replaced with her happiness and recovering the life that she lost. There is no doubt she's coming home, the unknown lies in the means that I have to go to to get her here.

April 6th, 2022, 10:33PM – I open the LINE chat as per my lawyer's instruction. The mediation session for the custody of Evelyn is set to ensue. I see a panel of lawyers, Evelyn's mother, Annie, and a court mediator. The hours leading up to this were the exact moments I had been preparing myself for. It wasn't the digital roomful of lawyers some eight thousand miles away, it was the insatiable urge and visceral taste of methamphetamines on my tongue. The lingering effects of the drug have been known to last for decades, and I am but months clean. The difference in my cleanliness is palpable, however. I am, and have been, in an all-out-war against my addiction to the drug. It is and has been the single hardest thing I have ever done in my life, and something I pray dissipates as time goes on. Every saliva bubble that runs its way from the tip of my tongue down my throat has a taste of meth. It scares me to the point of unsure, I question my own abilities internally, but I would never let anyone see that or know that. It makes me ponder scenarios where the drug would be welcome in my sobriety. It isn't, however. It will never be again. Sometimes I silently mouth those words to myself in hopes that I believe them, knowing that my words have held such a minuscule measure of integral weight in the past. The cries from my stomach are ones of a dying part of me. "The other guy" is kicking and screaming because he recognizes the moments where he shined through and coaxed us back to misery, only now, he has fallen on deaf ears.

As the panel of lawyers begin their dialogue in Thai, I jot notes on the frayed three-subject notebook that lay face up on my lap. Bits and pieces are all I can pick up, but it's irrelevant, as I know there is no such understanding of mediation and fair practice in Thailand.

As the hours go on into the morning of April 7th, I have dodged another 1440 of cravings and held my ground in my addiction's attack on my state of vulnerability. Evelyn is still down and displeased at the whole situation. The years she had known were normal as far as she knew. Annie and I had maintained a coparenting relationship that yielded success for Evelyn. Now, after being duped into a vacation and subsequently abducted, Evelyn has a noticeable discomfort in her speech and demeanor. The mediator even goes as far as to comment on it.

Throughout the entire mediation my lawyers are texting with me on a separate chat thread with as many compassionate words as possible. I remind them that this isn't about my feelings, but the life and future of my now 11-year-old daughter. This seems to take them back a bit as most parents seem to be in the custody battle for themselves; be it money or leverage. My entire life's purpose is contingent upon the happiness of this child. I can't find the words that help them see this clearly nor can I be within striking distance to whack them in the head with a baseball bat, but maybe we're both better off that way. My demeanor remained calm and my disposition and efforts were focused on making that one moment as beneficial to Evelyn's future as possible. I can't say my actions have always warranted or earned that statement, but they do today and they will for the rest of my life.

April 11ᵗʰ, 2022, 8:18AM – Before now it had been a comprehensible struggle identifying levels of desperation in my own mind and gut. The gut outweighs the mind, but we know it's ultimately the mind that will bring us back to a place of placidity. The gut will turn out our emotional insides and leave us for dead. The gut isn't on our side. The worst part is, is that there is no control over when the mind starts to outmaneuver the gut and get us back to ourselves, emotionally.

I have spoken to Evelyn a few times, all of which were guarded by her mother who has remained stoic and displaced in her attempts to quell our reunion. The lawyers have fought for this and I applaud and appreciate their efforts. It has brought us to an awkward what-can-I-say sort of awkward dialogue, and for me that is better than nothing, but nothing that is normal for either of us. We share the most intimate parts of our lives and realities to each other. Knowing we are one wisecrack away from termination is a thin line to walk, and one neither of us are willing to test. I'm just content to see her face looking back at mine. It's an irreplaceable moment. We talk about the animals and her school and how she's enjoying swimming. There is a tension in her, I can feel it. I can feel her unease by the way she glances up when she's about to talk as if she needs permission to speak. It infuriates me, but I can't let her know that. I make goofy noises like we would back in Boston and make fun of how Brady, our dog, has been behaving. Brady was an only fur-child before the other animals came along. Evelyn knows this and can pinpoint the moments in her mind. I see her connect the moments because I see a light in her eyes when she connects my words to our past reality. I can feel her contentment in her look. It's beautiful and frustrating at the same time. It's hope for me…. because I know I haven't lost her to hopelessness.

April 14ᵗʰ, 2022, All Day – How? Why? When? Where? I have the answers to none of these questions when it comes to my own child. The brief chat Evelyn and I had a few days ago is lingering in my mind. Her mother finally replied to a weeks' old email that proposed Evelyn returning to me in exchange for a lot of money; desperation in my part, I know. Nonetheless, it is just a symptom of my love. That's how I plausibly justify my desperation. Within any given 24 hour frame my mind wanders into thoughts of using meth and seeing Evelyn more than the minutes that pass. There is no justification for that or reason to need justification. It just is, yet both seem like pipe dreams to me. I caution myself on getting too high or too low with every one of those toxic thoughts, as they will both lead to my expiration if I chase either. I won't say the plan B strategy my mind implores me to take up is one that sees Evelyn's mother in an early grave, but I won't say it isn't.

April 25th, 2022 – 10:35PM – The tolls of empty-hearted days have been trumped by purposeful fortitude and perseverance. The hour has come to sit for the final mediation over Evelyn's rightful home and I'm perched at my computer, Tammy waiting in support to my right, waiting for the call to start. This has been the day marked for trial, but lawyers insist on never getting in front of a judge. I, however, see no other way. Once again we are met by stark refusal to allow Evelyn to come home, but there is a new development. Annie, surprisingly, has budged in her proposal. She asks off the jump if Evelyn may be allowed to come back to school in the United States at the age of 15. Fifteen years old and less than 60 days from her eleventh birthday seems way too long to allow my child to suffer unnecessarily for the enjoyment of her mother. Four more years of soulless video chatting while watching the anguish on my daughter's perfectly toned face is not a bargain at all. It's torture for Evelyn and for me. It's a hard "no."

Annie was expecting more and I hear her lawyer interject in Thai to remind Annie that it is my choice to go to trial. I am the plaintiff and she is the defendant. We will see each other in a few short months. August 10th, 2022 will be the culmination of my efforts to bring Evelyn home and reclaim my right as her father

August 9-10th, 2022. At the very beginning of my Southeast Asian jaunts, I would jump off a thirty-five-hour flight spanning over two layovers through three countries… and hit the streets of Bangkok running with some fierce heat and a pocket full of 'slush' money. That's what I call money that would be used specifically for getting fucked up and laid. Economy was the only class I could typically afford to fly, so as the years ticked on it became fitting that the trips wore me down more and more. The seats of economy class were cramped and smelly. Putrid at times. The congestion of airports and carry-ons way over the size limit pushed my frame to endure even more. Physically I could always endure more than the masses…considerably more. Emotional turmoil was something I never fully understood the magnitude of before Evelyn. Emotional distress is her gift to me. It's been a gift that lit my soul and sprouted integrity in the barren wasteland of a character I once ignorantly claimed to have. Somewhere along the line the trips of uninhibited bachelorhood and wild nights across whatever city in Southeast Asia called to me morphed into paternal desperation. Once Evelyn came along, the wild nights and ruckus adventures appealed to me about as much as a day in the kitchen pulling sphincters out of crawfish. Weird how you can want something, or someone so little and be so unprepared, yet the mere glimpse of their face pierces a ray of light into the soul that is more difficult to ignore than cancer...the thought of raising a white flag or accepting defeat in the saturated cloud of your child's disappointment is not on the ballot... and never will be. Having lost her whereabouts repeatedly through failed parenting I've become accustomed to coming back. The one thing I can't get over is having lost to another person. It's not as if I don't understand the magnitude of my ego, but if I take an honest glimpse of my purpose…my intentions are pure and predicated on Evelyn's happiness and opportunity. Ego, or Superego, as Freud claims, is my Achilles heel. It's my albatross.

Losing to another person or thing at anything to a man that knowingly and unapologetically takes every competitive edge he can, welcomes risk and lives fast…is off the table. What, or should I say who came to my 'table,' was Evelyn. She came and stayed. She loved harder than I ever saw a person love. She came and claimed her dad and offered me the life I thought I would never experience. She came and danced awkwardly and sang out of tune and coated my fickle, undeveloped heart with an impenetrable force field. Love.

Beyond the raw emotion is the day-to-day minutiae. Let's be real – even the most adventurous of us still has to accept a level of life's monotony. It's not like we have a molecular transportation device that ports us into the next adventure. Drama and exhilaration and more upon more are the symptoms of an unfulfilled soul. Evelyn and I both suffer from this affliction of hypo-mania , yet we can both accept the boredom as long as we're together. Enough may never be enough for either of us, but there is an unspoken understanding between us. *Let's get through this so we can experience that.* It's always a game of give and take. Maybe that's what brought such a heavy load on us...I know it is. We aren't great at giving so freely.

Tammy and I landed in Bangkok with a gut-full of nerves. This was Tammy's first trip out of the US, so the added stress and attention to her had to be balanced so as not to take away from the attention Evelyn's case was going to need without ostracizing Tammy from the moment and trial while she

adjusted to the twenty-seven hours of high altitude across three

countries and over ten time zones. A difficult feat for a man

with tunnel vision, but a skill I yearned to acquire over the

years. The only history I had to go off of was one that saw me

implode time and time again. Not this time.

August 10th saw the dawn of a lifetime. Tammy and I arrived at

court long before my legal team or Evelyn's mother. Tammy

and I sat outside in the clammy August heat of Thailand

rehearsing our testimony. We were prepared. As the courtroom

started to fill with lawyers, paralegals, translators, clerks, judges,

and Evelyn's mother…there was a noticeable absence. Evelyn

was nowhere to be found. She was subpoenaed to be there

months ago, but Annie had refused the letter. As infuriating as

this was we needed to be stoic and firm. I wavered, as showing

emotion to Thai people is a major sign of weakness and

emotional instability; things I've learned to use to my advantage after years of life throughout SE Asia. Tammy was asked to not even cross her legs as the judge may misconstrue her casual stance as complacent and presumptuous.

As the trial opened, it was clear from the start that we were getting the benefit of the doubt from the judge. He seemed to favor us. The trial was held in Thai language making it harder for me and impossible for Tammy to grasp. We answered question after question with confidence and let the translator do her best to convey our passion for Evelyn's justice. Stacks of evidence supporting Evelyn's progression and successes in the US were presented. As the trial concluded, lawyers and judges convened to discuss the outlying fact that Evelyn had experienced life in the US and thrived, but how could an indigent court withdraw a mother's right without testimony from the child? The judge was open but unwilling. It was a decision so far-fetched to Thais that it would have caused a ripple in the integrity of the kingdom of Thailand as far as custody battles with foreigners go.

I was warned by my legal team that even if I won, I would have to sustain another year or two bereft of a decision to Evelyn's fate after Annie, Evelyn's mother, would appeal the decision. I had to make a hard decision; negotiate with the terrorist to get Evelyn home and compromise a portion of pride I clung to, or forego up to two more years of speaking to and seeing my child for the sole purpose of winning. An ultimatum was discussed. We would find common ground in that everyone accepted that Evelyn would be better off in the US with us. Money was now the deciding factor as it was all Annie now had to bargain for.

Ultimately, the judge ordered Evelyn home the following Spring. She would finish out the year at her school in Bangkok that she was just enrolled in and come home soon after. We won. It would cost me around $20,000 dollars, but Evelyn had no price…not to me. Annie on the other hand, facing defeat and appeals, finally caved. We rushed the decision of our agreement to the judge for subsequent approval and it was a matter of time. Only time. Evelyn would theoretically come home for the start of Junior High School and return prepared. She would be unequivocally mine from then on. I'd love to tell the story of a hero father that swooped into a fiery wreck and swung his daughter to safety and lived happily ever after, but my happily ever after, as I've said, comes in the conformity of my soul to the universe. Evelyn was ordered return to the US the following year after she finished fifth grade, a year behind her peers. Regardless of what grade she entered and the hardships created by the last year, we won. Evelyn won her father back and I won the right to go on with purpose. Evelyn has always been my purpose.

Walking out of the courthouse I heard a voice behind us. *Evelyn wants to see you,* Annie said as she approached us hurriedly from behind. Evelyn was actually sitting in the car guarded by extended Thai family members I had never met throughout the trial. She popped the door open as I approached the tinted glass of Annie's passenger window and jumped out of her mother's car with arms wide open. It had been nine months since our attempted escape from Bangkok and Annie. We engulfed each other with an outpouring of desperation and the deepest sense of gratitude. We squeezed each other. I closed my eyes for a brief moment hoping to never forget the moment and feeling, never considering that I would need massive head trauma to ever forget what it took to get to that point. We sobbed profusely down each other's cheeks, rubbing our boogers unapologetically on each other while promising to never leave each other again. She was my home and I was still hers.

There are so many things I could point to with criticism in my own actions. I've learned that beating myself up is simply my inner child trying to get an ear leant to me. Evelyn is starting to understand this. Our words are just what we want our peers to think, our actions set us apart from our words, paradoxically. Reactions are just that, but responses are welcome. Talking about doing things makes me want to vomit unless it's followed with movement. I move. Stagnation is the devil's playground and my brain is not prepared for his shit…or her shit.

Then, we stood at the end of our current timeline – lost and unsure of what lies ahead. My gut told me this isn't over. I've become accustomed to expecting a difficult path because I see only one path. The loftiest perches are reached when I stop looking at the top and place my focus on the present position. History has sent my head in that negative orbit. My projected 'truth' is an algorithm that measures the past and divides it by the results after the efforts to change are subtracted from the principle. It's maddening but real. Acceptable but refused. Our fate was one handed down by the courts in Thailand. We have to wait and maintain. I have to exceed exponentially anything I've ever accomplished in order for Evelyn to come home, but it's an easy task when it's nonnegotiable.

The most perplexing part of my story came immediately after the decision by the Thai court. Reveling in victory is a dangerous place for the addict in me, and it, he, didn't miss his chance. As Tammy and I returned to Bangkok victorious that night, "the other guy" came rifling through me in a way I hadn't even bothered to anticipate. Laying in our room my head was no longer mine. He crept in and consumed me. With five days left on our mission I was left in a cold sweat laying next to my wife while my inner demons screamed at me in a voice so loud it was impossible to ignore. It was as if he was dying and saw an opening.

As night inched on I lay awake in visible turmoil while Tammy tiptoed around my peculiar mood. My head was consumed...fire, burn, burn, rage. *Go get those fucking drugs and celebrate the year you had, Matt,* he cried! I listened...I picked up my phone and opened an old application to seek a dealer in Bangkok. He read my message immediately. He was an instant yes to my request for a bag of meth. I was ready. "The other guy" had taken his shot and won. I frantically paced around the hotel room unsure of how to break the news to Tammy, Tammy, now in tears bellowed for me to come back to reality... *I'm fucking outta here,* "the other guy" exclaimed! I gripped the door and swung it open. I was about to hit the streets running. It wasn't as if I could bear my soul in weakness to my wife after a year sober. It was too embarrassing for the real me.

Just as "the other guy" got me alone in the hall of my hotel I was free to burn the city down for the night and hopefully crawl my way back in the morning as I had done so many times throughout my life. I got to the elevator...*go, go, go,* He barked and rejoiced. I started to map out my night internally. It felt good with a palate full of excitement. I was eerily full of energy after everything that took place during the entire, emotional year leading up to that day. .

As I saw a reflection of myself in the bronze panel of the hotel elevator door...I realized something scary. I had no idea who was looking back at me. All the fear in the world couldn't bring me back, but something did. Fear is and always will be the great equalizer, but I never had as much to lose as I had then. Everything would be gone in an instant. Evelyn would be a pipe dream that I had already won back. I would be giving her back to the world she loathed, willingly. *What the fuck was this entire year for,?* I asked myself. I was enraged at the feeling I had. *How could this be happening? Why did I deserve this?* The perpetual victim of my addicted headspace asked.

I let the elevator door open and close…pacing back and forth, now in tears myself. The amount of strength needed to be summoned was something I had never experienced until then. I hadn't even used yet, but I felt as though the drugs were already in me. "The other guy" presented my feeble mind with innumerable options for the evening, all of which somehow seemed plausible and fatal at the same time. I was gone. I'll never be able to fully understand what came next. Whether it was divine intervention or a strength I hadn't ever known existed…I turned and dragged "the other guy" back down that hall. I knocked, reluctantly on my own hotel room door. The door swung open immediately. Tammy was sobbing and visibly exhausted. I turned us in, myself included. Knowing the next few hours would be a torturous few didn't matter. I knew it was the fight of my life and I was now all-in. Tammy was always all in. Having a team of people in my corner has been the difference. The past year I put together had brought not only hope to me and Evelyn, but to the onlookers that waited with hopeful anticipation of seeing Evelyn come home. To those that preach connection, keep it up. I can't ever keep my guard so low again and I know that. The emotionally exhausting year leading up to the trial was so depleting that I had forgotten I was an addict for a moment. That's all "the other guy" needed. Never again.

For the first time in my life I openly admitted my own perceived weakness in needing help before needing forgiveness. Paradoxically, that is a far more courageous and rewarding path. I had come full circle. I won, for now. Winning doesn't always feel great and I learned that the hardest way a human ever should; shivering in a cold sweat of withdrawal one year removed from taking any drugs. That is how powerful addiction is, and I finally respected it enough to join forces in order to beat it. The most important lesson I've learned through my process of recovering has been the acceptance of self-doubt and the acceptance that I may not be qualified to handle all of life's curveballs alone. The understanding in my soul that I may not have the strength to handle everything, and that is okay. I'll never fully accept this as normal or necessary in my gut, but I'm willing to practice it steadfastly. My purpose is stronger now than my affliction ever was.

www.ingramcontent.com/pod-product-compliance
Lightning Source LLC
Chambersburg PA
CBHW071051040426
42443CB00013B/3303